ZEPHANIAH

VOLUME 25A

THE ANCHOR BIBLE is a fresh approach to the world's greatest classic. Its object is to make the Bible accessible to the modern reader, its method is to arrive at the meaning of biblical literature through exact translation and extended exposition, and to reconstruct the ancient setting of the biblical story, as well as the circumstances of its transcription and the characteristics of its transcribers.

THE ANCHOR BIBLE is a project of international and interfaith scope. Protestant, Catholic, and Jewish scholars from many countries contribute individual volumes. The project is not sponsored by any ecclesiastical organization and is not intended to reflect any particular theological doctrine. Prepared under our joint supervision, THE ANCHOR BIBLE is an effort to make available all the significant historical and linguistic knowledge which bears on the interpretation of the biblical record.

THE ANCHOR BIBLE is aimed at the general reader with no special formal training in biblical studies; yet, it is written with the most exacting standards of scholarship, reflecting the highest technical accomplishment.

This project marks the beginning of a new era of cooperation among scholars in biblical research, thus forming a common body of knowledge to be shared by all.

William Foxwell Albright
David Noel Freedman
GENERAL EDITORS

THE ANCHOR BIBLE

ZEPHANIAH

◆

A New Translation
with
Introduction and Commentary

ADELE BERLIN

THE ANCHOR BIBLE

Doubleday

New York   London   Toronto   Sydney   Auckland

THE ANCHOR BIBLE
PUBLISHED BY DOUBLEDAY
a division of Bantam Doubleday Dell Publishing Group, Inc.,
1540 Broadway, New York, New York 10036

THE ANCHOR BIBLE, DOUBLEDAY, and the portrayal
of an anchor with the letters AB are trademarks of
Doubleday, a division of Bantam Doubleday Dell
Publishing Group, Inc.

Library of Congress Cataloging-in-Publication Data

Bible. O. T. Zephaniah. English. Berlin. 1994.
    Zephaniah : a new translation with introduction and commentary /
Adele Berlin.
        p.   cm.—(The Anchor Bible ; 25A)
    Includes bibliographical references and indexes.
    1. Bible. O. T. Zephaniah—Commentaries. I. Berlin, Adele.
II. Title. III. Series: Bible. English. Anchor Bible. 1964 ; v.
25A.
BS192.2.A1   1964.G3   vol. 25A
[BS1643]
220.7'7 s—dc20
[224'.96077]   93-37736
                                                    CIP

ISBN 0-385-26631-6

10   9   8   7   6   5   4   3   2

FOR TOBY

(*Genesis 24:60*)

CONTENTS

♦

Contents

PREFACE

◆

Writing a biblical commentary is always challenging, even when the book is small and relatively obscure. I have set myself the tasks of making the Book of Zephaniah intelligible to the modern reader and of offering a fair representation of modern and pre-modern interpretations. In the first task I have been only partially successful, for a few phrases remain unintelligible to me, as they have been to others since ancient times. The second task has involved selection, and here I have followed my own tastes, omitting what appeared to be the more fanciful or less convincing explanations. My work was made both easier and more interesting by the recent commentaries of Menahem Bolle, J. J. M. Roberts, and Ehud Ben Zvi, and by the research of Robert Haak and Marvin Sweeney. The exegetical sections are preceded by an introduction in which I reflect upon a number of theoretical matters which have bearing on the study of the Book of Zephaniah and on other books as well.

I thank David Noel Freedman for inviting me to prepare this volume and for his unflagging editorial acumen, which is legendary to a host of authors and students. Explicit credit is given to him on occasion, but at other times the points he raised have been incorporated into the discussion without acknowledgment. Ehud Ben Zvi has exchanged ideas with me in private communications and has given me access to his unpublished research. Robert Haak, Marvin Sweeney, and Greg A. King have done likewise, and I thank all of them for sharing their work with me. The General Research Board of the University of Maryland at College Park awarded me a semester grant during which time I completed the manuscript. I am grateful to the University of Maryland, and to my colleagues in the Department of Hebrew and East Asian Languages and

Literatures and in the Joseph and Rebecca Meyerhoff Center for Jewish Studies for their interest and encouragement. My thanks go also to Monica Blanchard, who welcomed me into the Semitics/ICOR Library of the Catholic University of America and helped to facilitate my research. I thank my son, Joseph, for preparing the indexes. My husband, as always, deserves the largest measure of gratitude—one that I can never fully express—for his constant encouragement and love.

Adele Berlin
September 1992

ABBREVIATIONS

◆

AB	Anchor Bible
ABD	*Anchor Bible Dictionary*
AION	*Annali dell'istituto orientali di Napoli*
ASTI	*Annual of the Swedish Theological Institute*
BA	*Biblical Archaeologist*
BAR	*Biblical Archaeology Review*
Ball	I. Ball, *Zephaniah. A Rhetorical Study*
BHK	Biblia Hebraica Kittel
BHS	Biblia Hebraica Stuttgartensia
BT	*The Bible Translator*
BZ	*Biblische Zeitschrift*
BZAW	Beihefte zur ZAW
CAD	*Chicago Assyrian Dictionary*
CBQ	*Catholic Biblical Quarterly*
DJD	*Discoveries in the Judean Desert*
DNF	David Noel Freedman (personal communication)
GKC	*Gesenius' Hebrew Grammar*, ed. E. Kautzsch, tr. A. E. Cowley
ET	*Expository Times*
HAR	*Hebrew Annual Review*
HUCA	*Hebrew Union College Annual*
HVS	M. O'Connor, *Hebrew Verse Structure*
IB	*Interpreter's Bible*
ICC	International Critical Commentary
IDB	*Interpreter's Dictionary of the Bible*
IDBSup	*Interpreter's Dictionary of the Bible, Supplementary Volume*

IEJ	*Israel Exploration Journal*
JAOS	*Journal of the American Oriental Society*
JARCE	*Journal of the American Research Center in Egypt*
JBL	*Journal of Biblical Literature*
JNES	*Journal of Near Eastern Studies*
JNSL	*Journal of Northwest Semitic Languages*
JQR	*Jewish Quarterly Review*
JSOT	*Journal for the Study of the Old Testament*
JSS	*Journal of Semitic Studies*
KJV	King James Version
LXX	Septuagint
MT	Masoretic Text
NEB	New English Bible
NJPS	New Jewish Publication Society Translation
NRSV	New Revised Standard Version
RB	*Revue biblique*
REB	Revised English Bible
Roberts	J. J. M. Roberts, *Nahum, Habakkuk, and Zephaniah*
Smith	J. M. P. Smith, et al. *Micah, Zephaniah, Nahum, Habakkuk, Obadiah, and Joel*
TDOT	*Theological Dictionary of the Old Testament*
TQ	*Theologische Quartalschrift*
UF	*Ugarit-Forschungen*
v(v)	verse(s)
VT	*Vetus Testamentum*
VTS	*Vetus Testamentum Supplement*
ZA	*Zeitschrift für Assyriologie*
ZAW	*Zeitschrift für die alttestamentliche Wissenschaft*
ZDPV	*Zeitschrift des deutschen Palastina-Vereins*

A Note on the Transliteration

♦

For the transliteration of Hebrew consonants I follow the system preferred by *JBL*. In vocalized transliteration I do not use diacritical marks to distinguish vowels, for they complicate the printing process, are distracting to those who know Hebrew, and are not helpful to those who do not know Hebrew.

TRADITIONAL JEWISH COMMENTARIES CITED

♦

Abravanel. Don Isaac Abravanel. Portugal, Spain, and Italy. 1437–1508. A biblical exegete, philosopher, and statesman, Abravanel was well-educated in both traditional Jewish texts and in classical and vernacular literature. He was also familiar with Christian sources and interpretations. He produced an extensive body of biblical commentary in which he divided the text into sections and posed questions that he then proceeded to answer.

Ibn Caspi. Joseph ibn Caspi (or Kaspi). Provence and Spain. 1279–1340. A philosopher, grammarian, and exegete, ibn Caspi drew on his knowledge of languages, citing the Latin and Arabic translations of the Bible. His commentary is philosophical-theological and also pursues the literal meaning of the text.

Ibn Ezra. Abraham ibn Ezra. Spain. 1089–1164. Ibn Ezra was a poet, grammarian, exegete, philosopher, and mathematician. He may have written commentaries on all the books of the Bible, but not all are extant. His aim was to establish the literal meaning of the text. He included much philological and grammatical explanation and also drew on traditional material and his own experience of the world. His commentary is found in Rabbinic Bibles.

Kimḥi. David Kimḥi. (Also known as RaDaK.) Provence. Ca. 1160–1235. A member of a renowned family of scholars and translators, David Kimḥi was a grammarian and exegete. He wrote commentaries on Chronicles, Genesis, the prophetic books, and Psalms. He stressed philological analysis and the literal meaning. He also wrote a manual for copyists of the Bible in which he discussed the problem of *qere* and *ketiv*. His commentary is found in Rabbinic Bibles.

Malbim. Meir Loeb (Leibush) ben Yehiel Michael. Poland. 1809–1879. Malbim was a rabbi, preacher, and exegete who defended Orthodox Judaism against the Reform movement. He wrote a commentary on the entire Bible marked by emphasis on the literal sense of the text, linguistic expertise, and the exploration of the religious significance of metaphors and stylistic repetition.

Rashi. Solomon ben Isaac. Troyes, France. 1040–1105. The most well known of the medieval Jewish exegetes, his commentary on the Bible (especially the Pentateuch) and on the Babylonian Talmud enjoyed wide circulation. He included both literal and midrashic explanations, generally distinguishing between them. His commentary is found in Rabbinic Bibles.

ZEPHANIAH

MAPS

◆

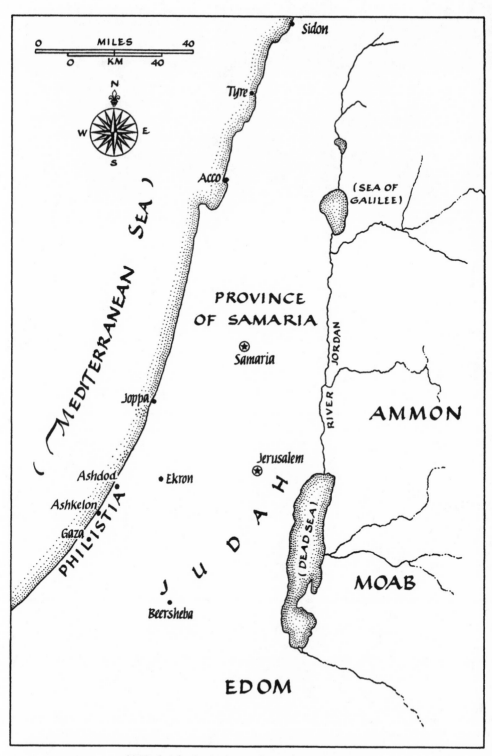

JUDAH AND ITS NEIGHBORS

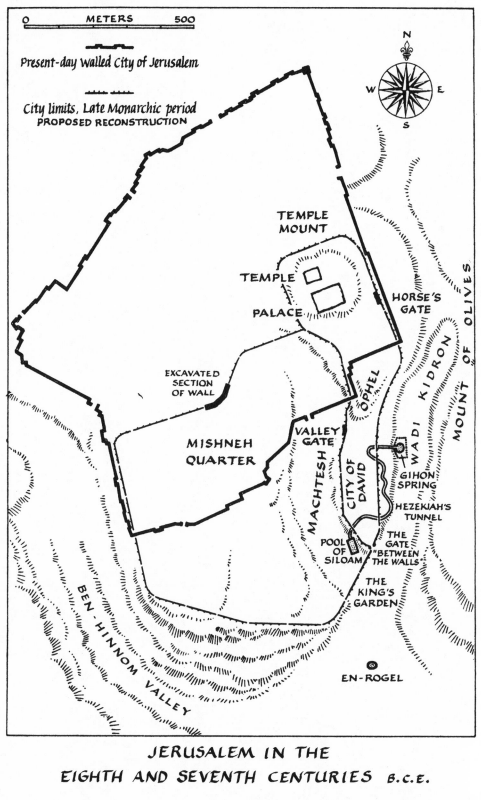

JERUSALEM IN THE
EIGHTH AND SEVENTH CENTURIES B.C.E.

THE BOOK OF ZEPHANIAH: A TRANSLATION

♦

I. SUPERSCRIPTION (1:1)

1:1 The word of the Lord which came to Zephaniah son of Cushi son of Gedaliah son of Amariah son of Hezekiah in the days of Josiah son of Amon, king of Judah.

II. THE ANNOUNCEMENT OF DOOM (1:2–9)

²I will utterly sweep away everything from upon the surface of the earth, says the Lord.
³I will sweep away humans and animals;
I will sweep away the birds of the sky and the fish of the sea, and the stumbling blocks along with the wicked;
And I will cut off humankind from upon the surface of the earth, says the Lord.
⁴I will stretch my hand against Judah and against all the residents of Jerusalem,
And I will cut off from this place every vestige of the Baal,
All trace of the idolatrous priests among the priests.
⁵And those who bow down on the rooftops to the host of the heavens,

1

And those who bow down, swearing loyalty to the Lord but
   swearing by their Melekh.
⁶And those who turn aside from after the Lord,
And those who do not seek the Lord and do not inquire of him.
⁷Hush before the Lord God for the Day of the Lord draws near.
The Lord has prepared a sacrifice, he has consecrated his guests.
⁸And on the day of the Lord's sacrifice:
I will punish the officials and the king's sons and all who wear
   foreign clothing.
⁹And I will punish on that day all who leap over the threshold,
Who fill their master's house with lawlessness and fraud.

III. A Description of Doom (1:10–18)

¹⁰And on that day there shall be, says the Lord,
A loud outcry from the Fish Gate,
And a wail from the Mishneh,
And a great crash from the Hills.
¹¹Wail, dwellers of the Makhtesh,
For gone are all the merchants,
Cut off are all who weigh out silver.
¹²And at that time I will search Jerusalem with lamps,
And I will punish the people who are congealing on their dregs,
Who think to themselves, "The Lord will not make things better
   or worse."
¹³Their wealth shall become pillage,
And their homes desolation.
They shall build houses but not inhabit them;
They shall plant vineyards but not drink their wine.
¹⁴Near is the great day of the Lord, nearing very swiftly.
The sound of the day of the Lord: bitterly shrieks then a warrior.
¹⁵A day of wrath is that day:
A day of distraint and distress,
A day of devastation and desolation,
A day of darkness and gloom,

A day of clouds and dense fog.
16A day of trumpet blast and siren,
Against the fortified cities and against the lofty corner towers.
17And I will bring distress upon people.
They shall walk like the blind because they have sinned against
the Lord.
Their blood shall be splattered like dust and their fleshy parts like
dung.
18Neither their silver nor their gold will be able to save them on
the day of the wrath of the Lord.
The entire earth will be consumed by the fire of his passion;
For a total, indeed terrible, end will he make of all the
inhabitants of the earth.

IV. THE LAST CHANCE TO REPENT (2:1–4)

2   1Gather together, gather like straw, O unwanted nation.
2Before the decree's birth—the day is fleeting like chaff—
Before there comes over you the fierce wrath of the Lord,
Before there comes over you the day of wrath of the Lord.
3Seek the Lord, all you humble of the land, who have performed
his command.
Seek righteousness, seek humility.
Perhaps you will be hidden on the day of the wrath of the Lord.
4For Gaza shall be abandoned,
And Ashkelon become a desolation.
Ashdod, at noon they will drive her out,
And Ekron will be uprooted.

V. PROPHECY AGAINST THE NATIONS (2:5–15)

5Woe, inhabitants of the seacoast, nation of Cherethites.
The word of the Lord is against you, Canaan, land of the
Philistines:

I will destroy you, make you uninhabitable.
⁶The seacoast shall be encampments of shepherds' pastures and
     sheepfolds.
⁷It shall be a portion for the remnant of the House of Judah
On which they shall graze;
In the houses of Ashkelon at evening they shall lie down.
For the Lord their God will attend to them and will restore their
     fortunes.
⁸I have heard the taunts of Moab,
And the insults of the Ammonites,
Who have taunted my people,
And made boasts over their territory.
⁹Therefore, by my life, says the Lord of Hosts, God of Israel,
Moab shall be like Sodom,
And the Ammonites like Gomorrah—
Clumps of weeds and patches of salt, a permanent wasteland.
The remnant of my people will plunder them,
And the remainder of my nation shall possess them.
¹⁰This is what they get for their pride,
For they taunted and boasted against the people of the Lord of
     Hosts.
¹¹The Lord is awesome against them,
For he shrivels all the gods of the land.
To him will bow, each from its place,
All the islands of the nations.
¹²Moreover, it is you, Cushites, who are the ones slain by my
     sword.
¹³And let him stretch his hand against the north and destroy
     Ashur,
And let him make Nineveh a desolation, arid as the desert.
¹⁴In it herds shall lie down, every nation's beasts.
Both the jackdaw and the owl shall roost on its capitals,
A voice shall shriek from the window—a raven at the sill,
For its cedarwork is stripped bare.
¹⁵This is the joyful city, dwelling secure,
Telling itself: I am the one and only.

Alas, she has become a desolation, a lair of wild animals.
Anyone who passes by hisses, shakes his hand.

VI. PROPHECY AGAINST THE OVERBEARING CITY (3:1–13)

3 ¹Woe, sullied and polluted, the overbearing city.
²She does not obey, she does not accept discipline.
In the Lord she does not trust, to her God she does not draw
    near.
³Her officials within her are roaring lions,
Her judges are wolves of the evening,
Who do not gnaw till the morning.
⁴Her prophets are audacious, people of treachery,
Her priests profane the holy, corrupt the teaching.
⁵The Lord is righteous in her midst,
He does no wrong.
Morning after morning he displays his judgment in the light
    which never fails,
But the wrongdoer ignores condemnation.
⁶I cut off nations, their corner towers were left desolate,
I turned their streets into ruins, empty of passersby.
Their cities were laid waste, empty of people, without
    inhabitants.
⁷I thought: Surely you will fear me, you will accept discipline.
And her dwelling will not be cut off, in accord with all that I
    have ordained against her.
But in fact they promptly corrupted all their deeds.
⁸Therefore wait for me, says the Lord,
[Wait] for the day when I rise once and for all.
For my verdict is to gather nations, to assemble kingdoms,
To pour upon them my anger, the full fierceness of my wrath,
For by the fire of my passion the entire earth will be consumed.
⁹After that I will turn over to peoples pure speech,
So all of them will invoke the name of the Lord,

5

And worship him with one accord.
¹⁰From beyond the rivers of Cush
  Atarai Fair Puzai will bring my offering.
¹¹On that day you shall not be condemned for all your deeds
        whereby you have rebelled against me.
  For then I will remove from your midst those elated with
        pridefulness.
  And you will no longer continue to be haughty on my holy
        mount.
¹²And I will leave in your midst poor and humble folk,
  And they shall take refuge in the name of the Lord.
¹³The remnant of Israel will do no wrong and will speak no lies;
  No deceitful tongue will be found in their mouths.
  Truly they will graze and lie down with none to disturb them.

VII. Joy to Jerusalem (3:14–20)

¹⁴Sing, Fair Zion,
  Shout aloud, Israel,
  Be glad and exult with all your heart, Fair Jerusalem.
¹⁵The Lord has commuted your sentence,
  He has cleared away your foe.
  The King of Israel, the Lord, is in your midst,
  You will no longer fear evil.
¹⁶On that day it will be said to Jerusalem: Do not be afraid;
  To Zion: Do not be disheartened.
¹⁷The Lord your God is in your midst,
  A warrior who brings victory.
  He rejoices over you with gladness,
  He keeps silent in his love,
  He delights over you with song.
¹⁸Those grieving from the festival whom I have gathered were
        from you.
  A burden on her, a reproach.
¹⁹Behold, I will deal with all your tormentors at that time,

And I will rescue the lame, and the strayed I will gather in.
And I will turn their condemnation into praise and fame
      throughout the whole earth.
[20]At that time I will bring you [home].
And at the time that I gather you,
Indeed, I will make you famed and praised among all the
      peoples of the earth,
When I restore your fortunes before your eyes, said the Lord.

INTRODUCTION

◆

THE CONTENTS OF THE BOOK OF ZEPHANIAH

> None of the prophetic books consists of complete speeches arranged chronologically, but rather of excerpts from different times in the life of the prophet, arranged according to topics; and, moreover, there is no transition between topics. For such is the power of the imaginative spirit of the prophet: to skip from topic to topic as it enters his mind, to put the later early and the early late, to speak about the nations and Israel together, to chastise the wicked and comfort the Godfearing. But all of them begin with punishment and end with comfort.

So wrote Max Margolis in the introduction to his Hebrew commentary of Zephaniah.[1] His words are, to a large extent, intended as a polemic against those who questioned the unity of the book, but they constitute an apt description of the Book of Zephaniah that we find before us. Zephaniah shares with many other prophetic writings an overall structure of chastisement followed by comfort—or, as modern studies often see it, a tripartite structure of judgment against Judah, judgment against the foreign nations, and a message of hope—and a similar range of subtopics and images through which this structure is embodied. But Zephaniah gives the impression, more than other prophetic books, of moving erratically between messages of chastisement

---

1. In Cahana, p. 73.

9

and comfort, and between descriptions of the fate of Israel and the nations.

The book opens with an announcement of doom upon the entire world. Humans and animals, birds and fish, are to be destroyed. Then the focus moves to Judah and Jerusalem, and to the idolaters there. They must prepare for the Day of the Lord, the time swiftly approaching when God will visit punishment on all who deserve it, including the members of the royal court and the merchant class who oppress the poor, and those who, in their complacency, doubt the power of the Lord. All these will be searched out from their homes in the wealthy suburbs of Jerusalem. Their wealth will become pillage, unable to save them; their settlements will be uprooted; and they will experience the darkness and devastation, likened to a battle and its aftermath, of the Day of the Wrath of the Lord. Chapter 1 ends as it began, with a picture of total destruction.

Chapter 2 modifies the total destruction by introducing the hope that at the last moment the humble of the land (the righteous who seek the Lord) will be spared. They will be sheltered when God's wrath pours over the Philistine cities to their west.

Two "woe" oracles follow. The first is addressed to the nations, beginning with the Philistines, moving to the Moabites and Ammonites, and then to Assyria. These nations will be destroyed and their cities turned into grazing lands for others or left empty and infertile.

The second "woe" oracle, which begins Chapter 3, is addressed to the sullied and polluted city, generally understood as Jerusalem. She is condemned because her leaders—officials, judges, prophets, and priests—have misused their offices. God's righteousness is contrasted with the corruption of these leaders. They have failed to learn from the destruction of the other nations and have continued in their arrogant ways. Now they, too, will feel the heat of God's wrath and will be destroyed. Afterward a humble remnant will remain. They will speak truly and take refuge in the Lord; and they will find peace and security.

The book ends with an ode to joy. Jerusalem will shout and exult, for her sentence has been commuted and her foes have been vanquished. God reigns supreme and victorious, and Israel has nothing to fear. The dispersed of Israel will be gathered in, their fortunes will be restored, and their fame will be known to all the world.

THE LANGUAGE AND STYLE OF ZEPHANIAH

In his essay on Jeremiah and Ezekiel, Joel Rosenberg notes that aside from meter and parallelism, Jeremiah's poetic style is marked by "staccato exclamations, rapid changes of scene and vantage point, frequent shifts of voice and discourse, use of invocation, plural command, and rhetorical question, a propensity for assonance and wordplay, a rich array of metaphors and similes from the natural landscape and from human crafts and trades, and precision of metonymy and synecdoche."[2] Such a description aptly captures the poetic style of Zephaniah no less than Jeremiah. This style, perhaps more correctly called an elevated rhetorical style, is not a formally metrical one, but does contain many poetic tropes and the rhythm that comes from the repetition of phrases and from parallelism. Many of the intricacies of Zephaniah's repetitions, word patternings, and rhetorical structurings have been charted by Ivan J. Ball, Jr.

It has been on the basis of parallelism, and to a lesser extent on meter, that modern scholars have deemed most prophetic speech, including Zephaniah, to be poetry, or, more properly, verse. More recently, M. O'Connor has proposed a syntactic definition of biblical verse (to replace what he calls the Standard Description stemming from Robert Lowth). O'Connor exemplifies prophetic verse by Habakkuk 3 and the entire Book of Zephaniah (*HVS*, 240–62). For those who espouse a metrical definition of biblical verse, Zephaniah has also been shown to qualify (see H. W. M. van Grol). Thus Zephaniah exhibits the characteristics of biblical verse, according to various (competing) modern definitions, although it was not so perceived in earlier generations.

Although Zephaniah draws on a common stock of images, he

---

2. Rosenberg, p. 185.

frequently achieves an added measure of vividness through an unusual turn of phrase or an uncommon term. For example, "foreign clothing" (1:8), "leap over the threshold" (1:9), "search Jerusalem with lamps" (1:12), "congealing on their dregs" (1:12), "their blood . . . splattered like dust and their fleshy parts like dung" (1:17), "gather like straw" (2:1), "In the houses of Ashkelon . . . they shall lie down" (2:7), "clumps of weeds and patches of salt" (2:9), "shrivels all the gods of the land" (2:11), "shakes his hand" (2:15), "wolves of the evening" (3:3), "pure speech" (3:9), "elated with pridefulness" (3:11). There is often extended description, as in the list of idolaters and syncretizers (1:4–6), the sounds of the destruction of the upper-class neighborhoods of Jerusalem (1:10–11), the Day of the Lord (1:14–16), the demolished Nineveh (2:13–15). Wordplay is prominent in 2:4, where the names of the cities echo their attributes. Anaphora is present in 1:3, 5–6, 15; 2:2, 3; 3:2. This style produces a concreteness of vision, which, together with the absoluteness of phrases like "I will utterly sweep away everything from upon the surface of the earth" (1:2), and the frequent occurrence of "all" in Chapter 1, gives the impression of very strong rhetoric. Various other types of repetition and patterning, discussed by Ivan J. Ball, Jr., and others, underline the literary nature of this book.

There are frequent and disconcerting shifts of voice in Zephaniah, from first-person address spoken by God to the third-person discourse of the prophet. So noticeable are these shifts that Paul R. House takes them as an indication of the basic structure of the book; he considers that the book is formed by dialogues between God and the prophet, and that its proper generic designation is therefore a drama. It is questionable, however, if we can speak of drama in ancient Israel, there being no evidence that this genre was known. It is better to view these shifts as a normal aspect of prophetic writing, since they occur in other prophetic books, too. The prophet conveys the words of God but he also interjects his own thoughts and reactions.[3] While the prophet fully identifies with

---

3. M. Greenberg, 160, calls this "subjective and objective language." J. A. Thompson labels this and other phenomena "responses" and finds them in prose, poetry, and prophetic writing. He includes in this category the antiphonal response, the chorus, the hymn, the liturgical formula, the refrain, the editorial comment, the gloss, the confessional statement, etc. To be sure, it resembles the type of responses found in drama or opera, but its presence is not limited to these genres.

God's message, he may step in and out of his role as God's mouthpiece. This actually strengthens the effect, because the prophet's own words confirm the words that he speaks in God's name.

ZEPHANIAH AND THE HEBREW BIBLE

The Book of Zephaniah is a study in intertextuality. A highly literate work, it shares ideas and phraseology with other parts of the Hebrew Bible to such an extent that at times it may appear as nothing more than a pastiche of borrowed verses and allusions. It may not always be Zephaniah who is the borrower, however, for the prophets who were his younger contemporaries or successors may have borrowed from him (or from the sources on which he drew). Specific instances are cited in the NOTES and COMMENTS. The general effect is the creation of a strong link between this otherwise obscure prophet and the rest of the canon—not only the Prophets, but also the Torah and the Psalms. Zephaniah participates in the textual world of the Hebrew Bible. This suggests that this textual world, in one form or another, was known and accepted by the book's first audience (whether that audience was in the time of Josiah or later), for only then would invoking it be rhetorically effective. While I am not the first to have noticed many of these textual connections, I emphasize them more than most interpreters because I find that they add an important dimension to the interpretation of Zephaniah.

Zephaniah and Genesis 1–11

Themes from the early chapters of Genesis appear in all three chapters of Zephaniah. Chapter 1 begins with a description that is a reversal of creation: human beings, animals, birds of the sky, fish of the sea. And, indeed, creation is being reversed; the created world is about to be destroyed. The phrase "everything from upon the surface of the earth" (1:2, 3—cf. Gen 2:6; 4:14; 6:1, 7; 7:4, 23; 8:8) reinforces the association with the stories of creation, expulsion from Eden, and the Flood.

13

Chapter 2, as I explain in the COMMENT, plays on the view of the world in Genesis 10. The prophecy against the nations, while a common component of prophetic writing, in this case is structured on the "geography" of the Table of Nations. It equates the nations with the sons of Ham, over whom the descendants of Shem will ultimately triumph.

Chapter 3 contains a hint of a reference to Genesis 11 in the phrase "I will turn over to peoples pure speech" (3:9), and in the emphasis on correct speech (v. 13) and the uniting of all peoples. It is as if the story of Babel were being reversed and all peoples reunited in the worship of the Lord. That others have seen this connection may be evident in the fact that in the triennial cycle of Torah reading (used in earlier times by Jewish communities in the Land of Israel and in Egypt), Zephaniah 3 is the prophetic reading *(haptara)* assigned to Gen 11:1 (see Ben Zvi, 24–25).

Zephaniah and Deuteronomy

There are a number of links between Zephaniah and the Book of Deuteronomy, as well as with the Deuteronomic History, especially 2 Kings. Zephaniah reflects the cultural milieu of the period from Hezekiah to Josiah and many Deuteronomic themes.[4] It pictures an expanded, wealthy Jerusalem, which may have resulted from an influx of northerners after the destruction of Israel in 722 B.C.E. and the times of Judean prosperity in the seventh century. Like the Deuteronomic writings, Zephaniah is strongly anti-syncretistic, viewing idolatry as the reason for the loss of the land and the exile of the people. The description of syncretism in Zephaniah 1 is very close to that in 2 Kings 23, and I have also found in it echoes of Deut 4:17–19.

Deuteronomy introduces the idea of the ban on the Canaanites, an idea which fits nicely with my interpretation of Zephaniah 2. It has an ideal picture of the extent of the kingdom, including transjordanian areas—corresponding to the Davidic borders and, as some see it, the territorial goals of Josiah. Zephaniah 2 may also relate to this geopolitical picture. Language and theme come together in the phrase *šwb šbwt,*

---

4. For details see Weinfeld, *Deuteronomy* 1–11, 25–62.

"restore the fortunes, return the captivity," a Deuteronomic phrase (Deut 30:3) which occurs twice in Zephaniah (2:7 and 3:20) as well as in Jeremiah and other prophets. Indeed, Zeph 3:19–20 sounds like an allusion to Deut 30:3–4 with its use of "the strayed I will gather in" and "restore your fortunes." And compare "praise and fame throughout the whole earth" with Deut 26:19. Finally, the punishments envisioned by Zephaniah in Chapter 1—banishment, blindness, loss of homes and vineyards, deserted streets, darkness, defeat—recall the curses of Deuteronomy, especially Deut 28:29–49.

Zephaniah and Prophetic Literature

The language of Zephaniah is closest to that of other prophets, especially Jeremiah and Ezekiel, who, according to their superscriptions, prophesied shortly after Zephaniah, and are also linked by modern scholars with the Deuteronomic school. There are also echoes of earlier prophets, especially Amos and Isaiah, and the later Deutero-Isaiah. The following list of phrases will give some sense of the extent to which Zephaniah's language and imagery participate in the realm of shared prophetic discourse. It does not include major themes or descriptions, which several prophets picture in similar terms, such as the Day of the Lord, images of destruction and dispersion, images of comfort and restoration, etc.

1:2 "I will utterly sweep"—cf. Jer 8:13.

1:3 "I will sweep away humans and animals . . . the birds of the sky and the fish of the sea"—cf. Hos 4:3.

1:7 "Hush before the Lord"—cf. Hab 2:20.

1:7 "The Lord has prepared a sacrifice"—cf. Isa 34:6; Jer 46:10.

1:9 "Fill their master's house with lawlessness"—cf. Amos 3:10.

1:12 "Congealing on their dregs"—cf. Jer 48:11.

1:13 "They shall build houses but not inhabit them; they shall plant vineyards but not drink their wine"—cf. Deut 28:30; Amos 5:11; Jer 29:5–7 and passim.

1:15 "A day of darkness and gloom, a day of clouds and dense fog"—cf. Joel 2:2.

1:18 "Neither their silver nor their gold will be able to save them on the day of the wrath of the Lord"—cf. Ezek 7:19.

2:2 "Fleeting like chaff"—cf. Isa 17:13–14.

2:3 "Seek righteousness, seek humility"—cf. Mic 6:8.

2:8, 10 "I have heard the taunts of Moab . . . This is what they get for their pride"—cf. Jer 48:29.

2:9 "Moab shall be like Sodom . . . a permanent wasteland"—cf. Jer 49:18.

2:14 "In it herds shall lie down, every nation's beasts. Both the jackdaw and the owl shall roost on its capitals, a voice shall shriek from the window"—cf. Isa 13:21–22; 34:13–15.

2:15 "This is the joyful city, dwelling secure, telling itself"—cf. Isa 23:7; 47:8.

2:15 "Anyone who passes by hisses, shakes his hand"—cf. 1 Kgs 9:8; Jer 19:8; 49:17; 50:13.

3:3 "Wolves of the evening"—cf. Hab 1:8.

3:4 "Profane the holy, corrupt the teaching"—cf. Ezek 22:26.

3:10 "From beyond the rivers of Cush . . . will bring my offering"—cf. Isa 18:7.

3:11 "Elated with pridefulness"—cf. Isa 13:3.

3:14 "Sing, Fair Zion . . . be glad and exult"—cf. Isa 44:23; 54:1; Joel 2:23.

3:17 "He rejoices over you with gladness"—cf. Deut 30:9; Jer 32:41.

3:19 "I will rescue the lame, and the strayed I will gather in"—cf. Mic 4:6–7.

Zephaniah and Psalms and Wisdom Literature

Since psalms, wisdom literature, and prophetic speech are all forms of elevated speech (some would say poetry), it is not surprising that they share some language. This is especially true when the same topic is discussed, e.g., "restore the fortunes." But, as E. Ben Zvi has observed, there are a few cases when Zephaniah's language seems especially close to psalms and/or wisdom literature—that is, Zephaniah uses terms or phrases which are relatively common in psalms and wisdom literature but rare in prophetic writing. For example, the "humble of the land" (2:3; cf. 3:12) has reverberations in Psalms 10, 22, 25, 34, 37, 69, 76, and 147, where the "humble" are mentioned or the root *ʿnw* figures. Also in Proverbs 15:33; 18:12; 22:4 one finds "humbleness, humility" (*ʿnwh*). The noun *ʿwlh*, "wrong," (3:5, 13) occurs in Ps 37:1; 43:1; 89:23; 107:42; 119:3; Prov 22:8; Job 6:29, 30; 11:14; 13:7; 15:16; 22:23; 24:20; 27:4; 36:23; it occurs only three times in the prophets: Mic 3:10; Hab 2:12; Mal 2:6.

The conclusion to be drawn from these resemblances to other parts of the Bible is not obvious, except to suggest that either the author or a later editor seems at home in a variety of styles of discourse that modern scholars assign to different schools and different times.

ON SUBDIVIDING THE BOOK OF ZEPHANIAH

The Book of Zephaniah is a short book, and, aside from the superscription which introduces it, there are no editorial insertions to suggest how it is to be subdivided. Its fifty-three verses could conceivably constitute one long chapter, yet they were divided into three chapters in the Middle Ages when the chapter divisions were made. Earlier, the masoretic tradition had divided the book into *pisqot*, but not all masoretic manuscripts are in exact agreement as to the number and placement of these *pisqot*. The chart below shows the divisions in the Aleppo Codex, the Leningrad Codex, the Cairo Codex, and the Petersburg Codex of the Prophets.[5]

---

5. Published facsimiles are as follows: *The Aleppo Codex* (Jerusalem: Magnes), 1976; *Pentateuch, Prophets and Hagiographa. Codex Leningrad B19A* (Jerusalem: Makor), 1971; *Codex Cairo of the Bible from the Karaite Synagogue at Abbasiya* (Jerusalem: Makor), 1971; *Prophetarum Posteriorum Codex Babylonicus Petropolitanus*, edited by H. L. Strack, 1876; reprinted by Ktav, New York, 1971.

Notice that the divisions in the Leningrad Codex differ from those in most printed Hebrew Masoretic Bibles, which divide Chapter 1 into 1:1–7, 8–9, 10–11, 12–18. The edition prepared by A. Dotan (Tel Aviv: Adi Ltd.), 1986, preserves the correct divisions. BHS indicates the *setumot* and *petuḥot*, the closed and open sections, but does not observe these divisions in its printed format, preferring to divide according to modern tastes.

ALEPPO	LENINGRAD	CAIRO	PETERSBURG
1:1–11	1:1–9	1:1–7	1:1–7
1:12–18	1:10–18	1:8–9	1:8–9
		1:10–11	1:10–11
		1:12–18	1:12–18
2:1–4	2:1–4	2:1–4	2:1–4
2:5–15	2:5–15	2:5–15	2:5–15
3:1–13	3:1–13	3:1–13	3:1–7
3:14–15	3:14–20	3: 14–20	3:8–15
3:16–20			3:16–20

Modern translations and commentaries differ considerably in their subdivision into sections. For example, to cite just two English translations, NRSV has seven sections while NEB has three major divisions and seventeen subdivisions:

NRSV	NEB (three major divisions)
1:1	1:1
1:2–1:13	1:2–3:10
1 :14–1:18	3:11–20
2:1–2:15	
3:1–3:7	
3:8–3:13	
3:14–3:20	

The Murabba'at text of Zephaniah is not sufficiently preserved to show all of the divisions, but it clearly begins a new section at 2:5 and 3:14. The Greek Minor Prophets Scroll from Naḥal Ḥever shows even less for Zephaniah, but this scroll agrees with the Leningrad Codex for the other prophets. (E. Tov, *The Greek Minor Prophets Scroll from Naḥal Ḥever*, shows that this scroll is a revised text designed to accord with the proto-MT.)

Commentaries show no more agreement, for example:

J. M. P. Smith	*J. J. M. Roberts*
1:1	1:1
1:2–1:6	1:2–2:3
1:7–1:18	2:4–15
2:1–2:7	3:1–20
2:8–2:11	
2:12–2:15	
3:1–3:7	
3:8–3:13	
3:14–3:20	

The lack of agreement in dividing so small a body of text is truly amazing. The locus of greatest agreement is in the chapter divisions, which correlate with the masoretic *pisqot* (although there are more of the latter). The chapter divisions seem to have influenced many, though not all, of the divisions made by modern interpreters. The masoretic *pisqot* are, as far as we can tell, apparently based on contents and often coincide with recurring structural or formal features; phrases like "and it will be on that day" and "woe" open *pisqot*. Modern divisions are usually based on contents and/or structural or form-critical considerations. Thus form and contents have served as the basis for ancient and modern subdivisions, though the way in which these are perceived may vary considerably.

My own subdivision follows the Leningrad Codex, with the exception that I have adopted the modern practice of separating the superscription from the body of the prophetic message and have treated it as a separate unit (the MT does not contain a break after verse 1). I follow the Leningrad Codex because it is currently the most well-known and widely accepted manuscript and because it contains the fewest subdivisions in Zephaniah. I want to make clear that these subdivisions are not meant to indicate compositional units. They are not intended to make a statement about the unity of the book, its genres, or its compositional history. I do not view the Book of Zephaniah as a collection of six individual oracles delivered on separate occasions and later joined together by an editor. The book as it stands, whenever it was written—in one sitting by one person or over many years by many people—now presents itself rhetorically and structurally as a unified work (with the possible exception of the superscription) and in its canonical form it was apparently intended to be interpreted as such.

THE EXEGETICAL APPROACH

I have tried to view the book as a unified work which conveys a coherent prophetic message. The NOTES contain philological and exegetical information on individual words and phrases. Although I had at first thought to make the NOTES as comprehensive as possible, I soon found that this was both impossible for me and impractical for the reader. The purpose is not to confuse but to clarify, so I limited the samplings to those that seemed the most reasonable, representative, or interesting. My aim is to explain to the reader how I arrived at my interpretation, and also, to a lesser degree, to give some sense of the recent history of the interpretation of Zephaniah.

A more discursive interpretation is found in the COMMENTS. Here I attempt to explain the meaning of the section as a whole, the interrelation of its verses, and its relationship to other parts of the book and to what I perceive as the book's message. At times I go beyond this to find links with other parts of the Bible or to discuss broader concepts that are important for the understanding of Zephaniah's words.

My approach is literary. I am searching for meaningful literary interpretations. I assume that a prophet's power is in his rhetoric, and that words ascribed to a prophet must not be trite or trivial. He must be saying something meaningful, and saying it in a manner that will have impact. Many prophets have a similar message, but each expresses it differently. A literary approach tries to get at the distinctiveness of a prophet's rhetoric and to explain how it achieves its impact.

For that reason I often object to certain analyses that fragment the book into its presumed original constituents, for by breaking up the text in this manner, a critic trivializes the units and may totally miss the overarching literary interpretation of a pericope. Take, for example, the "prophecy against the nations" in Zephaniah 2. Most biblical critics emphasize its similarity to other "prophecies against the nations" in other prophetic books, and some even note its differences, but few inquire how this passage relates to the rest of Zephaniah. Because they view it as having originated as a separate discourse, they tend to interpret it as such (even though sophisticated critics would admit that the pericope might have been designed from the start as part of a larger discourse). Regardless of whether it once existed separately or not, the refusal to interpret it in its present context diminishes the exegesis of Chapter 2.

The isolation of units is taken to an even greater extreme by those who find not one unit in the "prophecy against the nations" but many small prophecies against different nations. J. J. M. Roberts (195) explains that this passage

> consists of a collection of oracles against various foreign nations. Verses 4–7 are directed against the Philistines, vs. 8–10 are against Ammon and Moab, v. 11 is an isolated verse . . . , v. 12 targets Ethiopia, and vs. 13–15 are directed against Assyria. They have been shaped into a loose compositional unity, but there are indications that that unity is not the rhetorical unity of their oral presentation. The oracles reflect no common form, and there are no recurring patterns to tie them together.

This type of analysis is typical of those programmed *a priori* to discover small separate units. Roberts (9–11) views prophetic books as collections of oracles, analogous to collections of sermons, and stresses that one should not necessarily expect logical ordering or coherence in such collections. He takes the basic unit of interpretation to be the individual oracle (assuming that it can be isolated) rather than the pericope, chapter, or book as a whole. He sees little purpose in searching for a line of thought sustained or developed over several contiguous oracles because he views the ordering of these oracles as more or less random; or even if there is a logic to the ordering (chronological or thematic), it is secondary and not to be used in understanding the meaning of the original unit. Roberts' position puts the emphasis on the individual units, denying any purpose to the collector of these units other than a naive recording of them. In so doing, Roberts also denies or minimizes the existence of the book *qua* book, a work in its own right with a coherent design.

I find this difficult to accept because most if not all compilers, ancient and modern, have a purpose and seek to make their compilations coherent.[6] And most readers, despite Roberts' opposition to this practice, read as though the compilers did. By rejecting the claim that the juxtaposition of units affects their meaning, Roberts denies his readers a powerful interpretive device—the use of immediate context to make sense of an oracle. What Roberts is really telling us is to look only to the original context of the oracle, the prophet's first utterance of it, and to discount its present context in the prophetic book. But the original context is lost to us; we do not know exactly when, where, and why the prophet delivered a particular oracle. The only context we have is in the book. This secondary context may impart a secondary meaning to the oracle (for a thing may mean one thing in one context and another thing in another), but in the final analysis it is the context of the book that shapes and preserves the prophetic message. Moreover, the primary task of the exegete is to explain the *book*, not only its pieces. The exegete will therefore assume coherence (as readers do for all texts), until all attempts to find it fail.

I will argue in the COMMENT to Zeph 2:5–15 that there is, indeed, a powerful rhetorical unity in this section that can only exist if the entire passage is taken as a whole. Now I cannot prove that it was formed, *ab initio*, as a whole any more than Roberts can prove that it is a collection of separate oracles. I can only point to the fact that it exists now as a whole and there is no manuscript evidence that it ever existed otherwise;[7]

---

6. This includes ancient near eastern texts which may appear as nothing more than collections of raw data, like king lists, annals, lists of omens, and the like.

7. Form critics admit, sometimes begrudgingly, the "compositional unity" of such sections, but consider it of secondary importance (see Roberts, 162, 195). Ben Zvi (241–42) gives it slightly more weight in his comment on 3:11–13 and 3:14–15. He considers these two separate units but notices that they share similar language. He concludes: "Since these similarities can hardly be explained by blind chance, one has to conclude that, at least in [sic] the compositional level of Zeph 3:11–15, the two units have been related one to other [sic], and that the writer quite explicitly underscored the relationship between them by the use of similar language."

and that *viewing it as a whole yields an interpretation much more interesting and compelling than viewing it as a collection of separate parts.*

THE TEXT OF ZEPHANIAH: SOME THOUGHTS ON THE MASORETIC TEXT, THE ANCIENT VERSIONS, AND TEXTUAL CRITICISM

This volume presents a translation of and commentary on the Masoretic Text of the Book of Zephaniah. I have taken as my task the understanding of the MT because that is the received Hebrew text of the Hebrew Bible and it is the only Hebrew text that has been preserved in its entirety. Parts of the Bible have survived in Hebrew outside of the MT—among the Dead Sea Scrolls,[8] in the Samaritan Pentateuch, and in scattered Talmudic quotations of biblical verses—but none of these is as complete as the MT and the textual accuracy of all of them is no more certain, and in some cases a good deal less certain, than that of the MT.[9] Moreover, with the new spurt of publication and reexamination of the Qumran texts has come greater appreciation for the antiquity of the tradition behind the MT. According to L. Schiffman (*JBL* 111 [1992], 534), "it is clear that proto-MT was the dominant text form among Palestinian Jews already in the last two centuries BCE." All other premasoretic witnesses to the Hebrew Bible, such as the Ancient Versions,

---

8. From the area of the Dead Sea there survive a Hebrew text of Zephaniah from Murabba'at: 5 Mur 88 = Mur XII (Zeph 1:1; 1:11–3:6; 3:8–20) [Benoit et al., *Les Grottes de Murabba'at*, 50, 200–2]; remnants of a *Pesher* from Qumran; 1Qp Zeph (Zeph 1:18–2:2) and 4Qp Zeph (Zeph 1:12–13) [Horgan, *Pesharim*, 63–64, 191]; and a Greek translation from Naḥal Ḥever, 8Ḥev XIIgr (Zeph 1:1–4, 13–17; 2:9–10; 3:6–7) [Tov, *The Greek Minor Prophet Scroll from Naḥal Ḥever*]. These manuscripts date from the Roman period. They reflect the same order of the minor prophets and basically the same consonantal text as the MT.

9. Cf. the remarks by Weiss, *The Bible from Within*, 70, and Würthwein, 113.

are in languages other than Hebrew. Their place in the textual and exegetical study of the Bible will be discussed below.

The MT is privileged not only because it is the only fully preserved Hebrew text, but because it is the *textus receptus*, the accepted text of the Jewish and Protestant communities.[10] Even the Roman Catholic Church, in which the Latin Vulgate continues to be the official "authentic" edition of the Bible, has come to accept the MT as the basis of study for the protocanonical books of the Old Testament. (This began with *Providentissimus Deus*, 1893, and culminated with *Divino Afflante Spiritu*, 1943. See R. E. Brown, et al., *The New Jerome Biblical Commentary* [Englewood Cliffs: Prentice Hall, 1990], 1168–1170.) So even among Catholics, the MT has canonical status. For Jews and most Christians, then, and for biblical scholars of all persuasions, the MT is the basis for biblical study and interpretation. (The LXX is the accepted text of the Eastern Orthodox Church.) Textual critics, too, despite the MT-bashers among them, show, by their very acts of critiquing the MT, that the MT is the point of departure for textual study.

Is the MT an accurate text and does it faithfully transmit the original text? These are really two separate questions but they are not often kept apart by biblical scholars. The question of the original text has a corollary: Is it possible to know what the original Hebrew text was?

Textual critics have often assumed that the original Hebrew text of the Bible is retrievable or reconstructible, and they have set the reconstruction of the original text as their goal. But despite the considerable erudition brought to bear by textual critics, their reconstructions of the original Hebrew text remain hypothetical—educated guesses—and must remain so until actual written evidence of earlier stages of the Hebrew Bible is discovered. Moreover, when the various reconstructions and emendations are examined, wide divergences among them emerge. There are disagreements within each generation of scholars, but particularly striking are the disagreements from one generation to another. It turns out that despite what appears to be a continuity of methodology,

---

10. Early Protestant English translations of the Old Testament, such as the Tyndale Bible and the KJV, claim to have been translated from the Hebrew, although they were heavily influenced by the Greek and Latin versions.

there are distinct generational trends. For example, in a previous generation, there was a widespread tendency to emend *hitqošešu*, "gather together," in Zeph 2:1—most commonly to *hitbošešu*, "be ashamed of yourselves," or to *hitqaddešu*, "sanctify yourselves" (as in BHK). More recent commentaries have been less eager to emend, and have sought to interpret the given form (notice that BHS does not propose an emendation). This, and numerous examples of the same type throughout the Bible, suggests that textual criticism is not built on quite so sure a foundation as one might have supposed. It also suggests that regardless of claims about the priority that textual criticism should take over exegesis, the two procedures are not so easily disengageable. Emendations reflect the exegesis of the emender; emendation is the process of rewriting the text to make it say what the exegete thinks it meant to say or should have said. There are other influences at work, too, which act to encourage or discourage emendation. Among them are evaluations of the relative worth or reliability of the MT and the Ancient Versions, the amount of emendation to be tolerated, and the kind and amount of proof necessary to make a convincing case. In general, fewer emendations are made nowadays, largely, I think, as a reaction to the excesses of previous times in which a scholar's reputation was often enhanced by the cleverness of his emendations. In a reversal of the past trend, today's scholars see greater merit in finding an explanation for the words that are present than in substituting others of similar spelling. This does not mean that emendation is forsworn, but only that it is used as a last resort, when all other attempts to explain the text have failed.

But let us return to the question of the original text. It may seem that the quest for the original text eludes us for practical reasons, because of the limitations on our knowledge and the subjective influences on how we use the information at our disposal. But I would like to press further and pose the larger question of whether it is *theoretically* possible to find the "original" Hebrew text, or whether this is a goal that should be pursued. The question is not usually put so boldly, but there is evidence that it is beginning to be answered in a new way.

Let us examine several statements in text-critical handbooks. The first, by P. K. McCarter, is representative of what I will call the vertical model of textual criticism (which is still dominant in many circles). This model, which relates everything back to one original, is adopted with some modification by E. Würthwein. A different approach, which might be called the horizontal model, exemplified here by J. Weingreen, reflects a shift toward a newer theory of textual criticism.[11] Finally, E. Tov, the author of the most authoritative and intelligent discussion of textual criticism to date, aims for a balance between the extremes.

McCarter defines textual criticism as

> an enterprise that has as its objective the enhancement of the integrity of a text. It is based on the study of the extant copies of the text. The critic compares these copies and attempts to draw conclusions about the divergences between them. The goal is the *recovery of an earlier, more authentic—and therefore superior—form of the text.*[12]

Notice the confidence that the recovery of an earlier form is theoretically possible, and, what is more, that the earlier form is more authentic and therefore superior. McCarter counts among the extant copies to be studied the Qumran scrolls and the Ancient Versions. "Each of these copies," he tells us, "whether of the text itself or of a translation of the text, is called a *witness*, inasmuch as it provides testimony to the original form of the text." If McCarter assumes that the earlier form is the more authentic, then it is not surprising that he grants his earlier witnesses, the Qumran scrolls and the Versions, more credibility than his later witness, the MT. In fact, he argues against an *a priori* preference for the MT and an uncritical adoption of it even when it is intelligible and apparently not corrupt (pp. 13–14).

A similar position is taken by E. Würthwein, who, however, is less extreme in regard to the MT. He states that "in every instance it deserves special attention because it is based on direct transmission in the original

---

11. See the comments by J. A. Sanders in "Communities and Canon," REB, p. 99*.

12. *Textual Criticism,* 12. My italics. Compare Würthwein, 103, where he defines textual criticism as an attempt to "ferret out all the alterations that have occurred and recover the earliest possible form of the text." He explains that this cannot predate the canonization of a particular book.

language, and it has been handed down with great care" (*The Text of the Old Testament*, 113). He lists the MT as the first of the witnesses to be consulted (112), and applauds the abandonment of earlier tendencies to undervalue the MT in favor of the LXX or modern emendations (113).

A different view of the relationship of the MT to other witnesses is offered by J. Weingreen (*An Introduction to the Critical Study of the Text of the Hebrew Bible*, 6), who says

> Variant traditional readings account for a considerable number of discrepant readings found in duplicated texts in the Hebrew Bible itself, as well as in the renderings of the ancient versions and in readings of the Qumran biblical texts as compared with those in the massoretic Hebrew Bible. Often such variants may each have a claim to validity as much as the ones adopted in the massoretic Hebrew Bible. In such instances one might simply note these discrepancies without indulging in any subjective preference for one or the other.

Weingreen's point is crucial; he is suggesting that there is not one original text, but several variant texts (or "editions") each with its own claim to validity. When applied, this thesis leads to a comparison of the differences between the MT and the Versions—not for the purpose of dissolving their differences into an "original text," but for the purpose of understanding the effect of, and possibly the reason for, those differences.

This is a model which biblicists know from a different context. There is little doubt that the Books of Kings and Chronicles drew on the same material (or Chronicles drew on Kings); but no one seriously uses one to "correct" the other. They are two separate and distinct texts, each with its own agenda. The fact that they have material in common is less interesting than the distinctive use each has made of that material. The question to be posed to a comparison of Kings and Chronicles is not "What was the original text?" but rather "How can we understand and appreciate the differences in these works?"[13]

The implication of this approach for textual criticism is enormous,

---

13. This is the thrust of a few comparisons between the MT and the LXX. See, for example, M. Greenberg, "The Use of the Ancient Versions for Interpreting the Hebrew Text," *VTS* 29 (1977), 131–48; and S. D. Walters, "Hannah and Anna: The Greek and Hebrew Texts of 1 Samuel 1," *JBL* 107 (1988), 385–412.

for instead of a vertical model which creates a stemma leading back to one original text, we have a horizontal model which accords each text or text type independent status and legitimacy.[14] This means that there should be no search for the "original" text in the concrete sense of the very first draft. Whatever original text may have existed has long ago disappeared.[15] It existed for so brief a moment that its recovery is hopeless and meaningless. The earliest remains that we possess are variform realizations of the hypothetical original—in the form of pre-masoretic Hebrew manuscripts at Qumran and the translations of the Ancient Versions. They are not necessarily more correct forms of the one and only Hebrew original than the MT is; they are simply different realizations, or interpretations, of a *hypothetical* original. They are, quite simply, different texts. In some instances they seem to reflect a different *Vorlage* from the MT and in other instances they do not. Their relationship to the MT is certainly interesting and worthy of study, but they are not, *ipso facto*, more "correct" or more "original" than the MT.

The horizontal model not only changes our textual critical practices, but also reinforces what is being learned about the early stages in the process of textual transmission. This is not the place for a discussion of this complex issue,[16] except to note that it seems that in the Greco-

---

14. Peter Machinist pointed out to me that the same model is now operating in other areas. See, for example, Piotr Michalowski, "History as Charter: Some Observations on the Sumerian King List," *JAOS* 103 (1988), especially p. 243.

15. J. A. Sanders, REB, 98*, makes the point that it is senseless to try to recover a pre-canonical form of a text; Würthwein agrees. Sanders argues that biblical texts are the products and possessions of communities, not individual authors. This, he says, "should limit the tendency of western minds to push behind inherited texts in search of supposed original forms of texts composed by ancient individuals."

By implication, it is also meaningless to speak of one canonical form of a biblical book, for a book canonized in Hebrew for the Jewish community is not the same thing as the same book canonized in Greek or Latin for a Christian community. A comparison of the Hebrew and Greek Esther provides the most obvious proof that there is more going on between the LXX and the MT than textual corruption.

According to J. R. Davila's review (*JBL* 111 [1992], 512–13) of F. E. Deist, *Witnesses to the Old Testament: Introducing Old Testament Textual Criticism* (Pretoria: NG Kerkboekhandel), 1988, Deist espouses a position on the use of early witnesses similar to mine. I have not been able to obtain Deist's book.

16. On this subject see Sarna in *Encyclopedia Judaica* 4:832–36; Fox; and the work of E. Tov, especially *Textual Criticism of the Hebrew Bible*.

Roman period there were different Hebrew text types in circulation and that within certain communities at least, attempts were made to authorize a particular text type and safeguard its accurate transmission. Traces of these different text types are found in the early witnesses to the Bible. By the time of the Masoretes, it was no longer a question of selecting a text type but of accurately transmitting the one inherited. To correct the masoretic text type by means of a different text type is tantamount to replacing one community's Bible by another.

All of this leads me to conclude that while the concept of the "original text" may be useful at times, the "original text" is a will-o'-the-wisp, a hypothetical construct of which we possess multiple realizations.

This position, while not unheard of, is radical for textual critics—largely, I believe, because to accept it would require a complete redefinition of the goal of textual criticism. Therefore, while a textual critic may accept it on a theoretical level, on a practical level he or she will speak of an original text. This is the position taken by E. Tov, who admits that "the question of the original text of the biblical books cannot be resolved unequivocally" (*Textual Criticism of the Hebrew Bible*, 166) and that "the period of relative textual unity reflected in the assumed pristine text(s) of the biblical books was brief at best, but in actual fact it probably never existed" (189). Nevertheless, Tov accepts the concept of "one original text" with "the possibility of earlier, written stages" (189). Tov's "original text" is, then, an arbitrary point in the development of the Bible, but one that is necessary if textual criticism is to be practiced.

The textual criticism of the Book of Zephaniah does not uncover variants in the Versions pointing to a *Vorlage* different from the MT; and, in any case, the task of an exegete is to explain the MT. So the question posed to the non-masoretic witnesses by an exegete is not "What did the pre-masoretic book look like?" but rather "What is the role of the early witnesses in the exegesis of the MT?" *They should be viewed not as witnesses to a pre-masoretic stage of the "original text," but as witnesses to a pre-masoretic stage of interpretation of a hypothetical text which may or may not be the MT Vorlage.* In this they do not differ in principle from later witnesses, like medieval commentaries and modern translations, except that they are much older and, in the case of the Versions, have had a long tradition of influencing how the Bible was interpreted. All are, by definition, manifestations of biblical interpretation.[17]

Different translations, both ancient and modern, like different interpretations, should be brought into the discussion of a biblical text because they show how the text has been understood in the past. They often alert us to textual ambiguities or irregularities, which, like a grain of sand in an oyster, can grow into exegetical pearls. I cite the Ancient Versions and modern translations, as well as commentaries from medieval to modern times, when they shed light on the process of interpretation or when they provide interesting results. As I stated at the outset, I view my task to be to make sense of the MT, and therefore I have subordinated the other witnesses to it, even when they make better sense. The fact that they make better sense does not mean that they were reading from a more accurate text. It may only mean that their solution to a problem obscures the fact that they, too, had a problematic text. Ancient translators, like modern ones, are compelled to solve cruxes and decide between competing renderings. They make different choices, but their results do not prove that they had different Hebrew texts any more than the differences between, say, the RSV and the NEB prove that they were based on different Hebrew texts.[18]

This brings us back to the question of the accuracy of the MT. It is not a question of accuracy vis-à-vis a hypothetical original, but accuracy in respect to conveying intelligible thought through the conventions of biblical Hebrew. There are occasions when the MT fails to make sense, i.e., uses an unintelligible word or an anomalous grammatical construction. This may be due to miscopying on the part of the Masoretes themselves, or, more likely, to errors in the manuscripts upon which they relied.[19] The Book of Zephaniah contains a number of these instances. On such occasions scholars are especially prone to seek

17. This point is recognized by Tov, *Textual Criticism of the Hebrew Bible*, 123, 134, 295.

18. Cf. the remarks in Sasson, *Jonah*, 13 and Tov, *Textual Criticism of the Hebrew Bible*, 123, 132.

19. The Masoretes were conservative and would not have taken upon themselves to correct traditional readings, even if they were not fully intelligible.

remedies in the Versions (because they think that the Versions reflect less corrupt texts) and/or in emendations (because these make the text say what it should have said—sometimes the emendations follow the Versions and at other times they represent modern solutions). I seek out the Versions on these occasions because they represent previous solutions to the problem. As for emendations, I am in principle not opposed to making them, but the bigger the crux, the larger the number of solutions that is likely to be proffered. With the proliferation of possible solutions, my confidence in any one of them diminishes, and I must occasionally admit that there appears no possibility to restore what lay behind the MT. I deem it sufficient to call attention to possible corruptions or interpretive cruxes, citing previous opinions and solutions. At times I have a preference, or even occasionally a novel interpretation, and I will make that clear. At other times I am unable to decide, and so I leave it to the reader to choose among the options.

AUTHORSHIP, DATE, AND HISTORICAL SETTING

Who Was Zephaniah?

The superscription tells us that the words that follow it were spoken by a prophet named Zephaniah who prophesied during the time of Josiah, that is, sometime between 640–609 B.C.E. Outside of this one reference, there is no other mention of this prophet, even within the book itself, and thus no way to confirm whether he indeed existed and spoke the words attributed to him. His existence is credible, though, because other prophets like him were active before, during, and after this period, and because the personal name "Zephaniah" is an authentic name, found in the Bible (applied to several other individuals) and on a seal impression from Lachish.

Who Wrote the Book of Zephaniah?

Even if there was a prophet named Zephaniah, that does not necessarily mean that he was the author of our book. His appearance in the
superscription may be interpreted in several ways: (1) that he actually said
the very words that are preserved, (2) that he prophesied the general
contents of the book but a later editor rephrased his words, or (3) that he
is a fictive author, a speaking voice, or what literary critics call an implied
author. It is this last explanation which is beginning to appeal to some
recent scholars, for it dovetails with their literary approach and it keeps
open the question of the date of the book.

J. Rosenberg, speaking of Jeremiah and Ezekiel, puts it this way:

> A literary reading must try to make sense of how the books have chosen
> to unfold the words of their alleged authors, for it is fair to say that
> Jeremiah and Ezekiel are less the authors of their books than personages
> or voices within a text. Despite the common ancient practice of
> attributing authorship of a work to one or another chief figure within it
> (a practice that critical scholarship sometimes perpetuates), it is likely
> that ancient readers were at least subliminally aware of another pres-
> ence—anonymous, narrative, and traditionary in character—by whose
> intelligence the prophet's words acquired additional shape, coherence,
> and historical resonance for a later community.[20]

Rosenberg's "voice within a text" is a literary way of distinguishing
the speaker of the prophetic words within the text from the author of the
book.[21] Such a distinction does not directly address the question of
authorship, which in turn is bound up with the question of dating the
book.

---

20. "Jeremiah and Ezekiel," *The Literary Guide to the Bible,* eds. R. Alter and F.
Kermode, p. 184.

21. I appreciate this distinction, but despite Rosenberg's criticism, I will sometimes
continue the practice of referring to the author as "Zephaniah," or "the prophet," for,
since the author is invisible, he tends to merge in our minds with the speaking persona
in the text.

E. Ben Zvi (349–52), taking a more historical approach, also espouses the notion that Zephaniah is a fictive author, but that is because Ben Zvi dates the Book of Zephaniah to the post-monarchic period, hence a seventh-century Zephaniah could not have written it. For anyone who dates the book later than the Josianic period, Zephaniah is a fictive author and the book is a pseudepigraphic work, the work of a later author ascribed to an earlier prophet. Ben Zvi suggests that this format was adopted because in the post-monarchic period the words of an earlier prophet would have had more authority than the words of a contemporary prophet or spokesman. However, Ben Zvi does allow for a pre-compositional level which may have originated from a real Josianic prophet;[22] he thus mitigates the argument that the book is totally a later fabrication. Indeed, the total fabrication of an otherwise unknown prophet is difficult to imagine.[23] What authority would such a prophet have had? It seems better to take the middle ground: to acknowledge the activity (or at least the tradition of such activity) of a monarchic prophet named Zephaniah, who, in the book ascribed to him by a post-monarchic author or editor, became, in a literary sense, the implied or fictive author. Since the question of authorship cannot be divorced from the question of dating, we turn now to the dating of the book.

When Was the Book of Zephaniah Written?

The superscription places Zephaniah in the time of Josiah (640–609 B.C.E.). This date, of course, may be as fictive as the ascription of

---

22. See his discussion on pp. 291–95, 357–58. Ben Zvi accepts that pre-compositional material is reflected in certain units but rejects the notion that this material constituted one Zephanic source. He accepts "the existence of certain corpora of traditions commonly accepted as Zephanic prior to the compositional level" (357). In other words, Ben Zvi is not arguing that a post-monarchic author created the book *ex nihilo*. He is, rather, arguing against the existence of a transcript of a monarchic Zephaniah's words which formed the basis of the book. Whatever may have existed of a historical Zephaniah's words has left only a trace or a memory; the real credit of authorship belongs to the post-monarchic writer of the Book of Zephaniah.

23. So DNF. Note that the closest parallel, the Book of Jonah, lacks a historical superscription but uses as its protagonist a prophet mentioned in 2 Kings 14:25. The pseudepigraphic literature from Greco-Roman times is always attributed to known biblical figures.

authorship, but most exegetes have taken it literally and have devoted their energies to narrowing down the years during Josiah's reign in which Zephaniah delivered his prophetic addresses. Because the picture in Zephaniah 1 appears to correlate with the pre-reform description in 2 Kings 23, the consensus is that Zephaniah was active during the early years of Josiah, before the institution of his religious reforms in 622 B.C.E. (Roberts, 163, is representative of this position.) Many see the prophet as a supporter of religious reform, and perhaps even of Josiah's political policies (Christensen). Furthermore, the lack of mention of the king in 1:4–9, and the mention of the "sons of the king," has been taken as evidence that Josiah was still a minor at the time. The description of Assyria in Zephaniah 2 gives the impression of a still-mighty power which the prophet can visualize being destroyed, and so may correlate with the time before the death of Ashurbanipal in 627 B.C.E. Philistia, Moab, and Ammon were vassals of Assyria and were destroyed or subjugated by the Babylonians shortly after Assyria's fall. So the geopolitical picture in Zephaniah 2 correlates with that of the late seventh century. A number of similarities with the Deuteronomic history in language and theme (see above) have reinforced the sense that the Book of Zephaniah was the product of the Deuteronomic school, which is also dated by many to the Josianic period. And the absence of references to later events (the rise of Babylonia or Egypt) has clinched this dating in the minds of the majority of scholars.

A few scholars, however, prefer a date later than 622 for all or parts of the book: E. Achtemeier dates most of Chapter 3 to 612–609, the end of Josiah's reign; J. P. Hyatt and D. Williams both date the entire book to the reign of Jehoiakim, 608–598 (the reforms of Josiah having failed); B. Peckham estimates that the book's first edition was ca. 590; and L. Smith and E. R. Lacheman suggest that it was composed as late as 200 B.C.E. (although this last opinion has found little support).

A strong case for an unspecified post-monarchic date has been made recently by Ben Zvi. Among the arguments that he marshals are evidence of later linguistic and thematic usages (for example, similarities to exilic or postexilic psalms, and the genealogies in Ezra and Nehemiah), and the late dating of most of the latter prophets. Most important, he offers a scenario according to which the book would have been more meaningful in a post-monarchic period than it would have been during the late monarchy.

Several of Ben Zvi's observations deserve notice because they raise points not usually considered in discussions of the dating of Zephaniah.[24] Classical prophecy reached its peak during the monarchy; most prophetic books, regardless of when they were actually written, are ascribed to prophets who lived during the divided monarchy.[25] Hence it would seem that monarchic prophets have the highest status and authority, and therefore it would have behooved a later author to attribute prophetic words to a monarchic prophet.

According to this view, the author of Zephaniah, who was not the prophet, got his legitimacy not from a direct divine revelation but from the apparently faithful transmission of an earlier revelation.[26] From the point of view of the prophet, his prophecies are as yet unfulfilled; but from the point of view of the author and his audience, who lived at a later time, the prophecies of judgment have been fulfilled (Assyria and its vassals have been destroyed) and the prophecies of salvation await fulfillment (the humble remnant of Judah will regain security). The prophetic message gains credibility with this exilic audience because parts

---

24. There are implications for the dating of other prophetic books, too. For a concise discussion of the criteria for dating, applied to Jonah, see Sasson, *Jonah*, 20–28.

25. The best example is the Book of Jonah. The book lacks a superscription and its date is unknown, though there are good arguments for placing it in the exilic or postexilic period (see Sasson, 20–28); but its "hero" is a prophet mentioned in 2 Kgs 14:25, a prophet from the time of Jeroboam II. (And Nineveh/Assyria figures prominently in both Jonah and Zephaniah.)

There are, however, major differences between Zephaniah and Jonah. The genres of the books are different and there is no suggestion that Jonah wrote the book bearing his name. Rather, it presents itself as a third-person narration by an anonymous author about Jonah.

26. Compare the comment of J. Blenkinsopp, *The Pentateuch*, 234: "If the first collection of prophetic writings was put together during the exilic period by the same school that produced Deuteronomy and Dtr [the Deuteronomic History], a hypothesis which has much to recommend it . . . [t]he existence of an official corpus of prophetic writings would not in itself exclude ongoing prophetic activity, but it would tend inevitably to shift the emphasis from the present to the past, from the spoken to the written word, and from direct prophetic utterance to the interpretation of written prophecies."

of it have already come to pass, intimating that the rest will also come to pass.

The author of Zephaniah, according to Ben Zvi (353), was influenced by other prophetic traditions, wisdom literature, the ʿanawim psalms, the malak psalms, and congregational psalms. The image of the ideal community in the book is one of poor and humble people without a king or a royal elite, oppressed by wealthy, proud, impious enemies. The community awaits salvation from God alone—no king or national leader is expected to arise. The book was presumably written for an audience which could identify itself with this ideal community. That audience is, in Ben Zvi's words, one which could "understand itself as a post-monarchic group whose horizon and focus is [sic] not that of creating (or recreating) a political center of power, a new and just bureaucracy" (356). Instead, this group focuses on religious attitudes, such as reliance on God, humbleness, and the knowledge that God is just and there will come a time when the ideal world will become a reality. Ben Zvi thereby portrays a community that has accepted its subordinate status, has given up hope of political autonomy, and must concentrate on building its religious identity and sustaining hope for its future continuity. That community sounds like the exilic community before the advent of the Persian empire and the opportunity for restoration.[27]

Ben Zvi's suggestion of a post-monarchic date has yet to be thoroughly evaluated. Against it is the picture of syncretism in Chapter 1, a problem that was common in the monarchic period and not at all in the postexilic period.[28] It is not known whether the exilic community was troubled by this phenomenon.

Another objection might be the omission of Babylonia. But this might be explained in the same way as the omission of Egypt; namely, that Babylonia had not yet fallen and it was crucial to enumerate

---

27. Ben Zvi also speaks of a post-compositional level (358), from the time of writing until the text became fixed.

28. Ben Zvi considers this part of the pre-compositional level. But it is hard to see why it would have been included by a later author. Alternatively, it could be viewed as a bit of verisimilitude, calculated to give authentic flavor to the Josianic setting. But this may ascribe too much modern literary sophistication to an ancient author.

destroyed nations in order to show that the prophecy had come true. The Assyrian setting accomplishes this.

My sense is that whether or not Ben Zvi is correct, he has provoked some thought about the process by which scholars date prophetic books and the assumptions which underlie that process. Dating a book is important for interpreting it, for without knowing the context from which a work sprang, we cannot understand its full impact. Although much in the Bible is timeless, its texts are the products of historical events and circumstances, and they become clearer and more meaningful if we can pinpoint the occasions that gave rise to them.[29] But here we enter a hermeneutic circle, for we often arrive at the dating based on our interpretation of the text; and, at the same time, our interpretation is informed by our assumption regarding the date.[30] To break out of this hermeneutic circle is difficult, if not impossible, but it may help to refocus the question. Instead of asking when this book was written, we should ask what would it have meant to a Judean audience during the time of Josiah, or to a Jewish audience in exile in Babylonia, or to a Judean audience in the time of Ezra, and so forth. We have to ascertain the meaning of the book's message as best we can and then try it out, as it were, to see which period it would fit best. Most biblical scholars do this to some degree. Ben Zvi has done it more explicitly and has arrived at a conclusion different from the current consensus. While he does not offer a precise date, he concludes that the book's message (as he interprets it) would have been most meaningful to a post-monarchic audience. Hence, concludes Ben Zvi, that was when it must have been written.

But, some exegetes will object, in this case the book tells us in its

---

29. This position is counter to New Criticism and various structuralist and post-structuralist schools that interpret a text without regard for its original context. More recent literary criticism has returned to a concern for the context of a work and the ideology that may be embodied in it.

On the relationship between dating and interpretation note the remarks by Sasson, *Jonah*, 27: " 'To date' a particular document to a specific period . . . should fulfill at least two reciprocal functions: first, the intellectual positions of the period to which it is assigned ought to clarify the text; and second, the text should inform us about the period in which it was created."

30. A parade example is the Book of Ruth, which means something quite different if it is dated to the early monarchy or dated to the time of Ezra.

superscription that it was written during the time of Josiah. Here, perhaps even more than in his conclusion, I find that Ben Zvi's approach offers a new way of looking at prophetic superscriptions. Most biblicists take them as the work of later editors giving accurate historical information about their prophetic source. (It is interesting to note the inconsistency whereby scholars can dismiss the superscriptions of psalms as fanciful, yet take the prophetic superscriptions seriously.) Ben Zvi's analysis raises the possibility that the superscription is not the work of a later editor, but is by the same author as the rest of the book; and, furthermore, that its function is not to provide us with historical information but rather to provide a setting for the book. This view derives from his "historical-critical" analysis, yet it is remarkably similar to the way a literary interpretation might see it; namely, that the author has chosen a prophetic persona as the implied or fictive author of the work, and has set the work in the period of this prophetic persona. The real author is sending a message to his audience by means of a fictive author from an earlier period. Or, since it is difficult to assume that an author could create a prophet out of whole cloth, the real author is reinterpreting, in his own words and for his own purpose, earlier prophetic material. Prophetic books should not be seen as naive recordings of prophetic utterances—unmediated artifacts; they are, rather, sophisticated retellings or reinterpretations, mediated by an author or editor, for an audience different from the original prophet's and presumably for a different purpose.

The point to be grasped here is that the time of Josiah is not necessarily the time that the book was written, but it is *the time in which the book is set*. The book clearly presents itself as being set in that period; it is meant to be understood against the background of the latter part of the seventh century B.C.E. An exegete must take the historical setting seriously, not because it holds the secret to the book's date, and not even because it is a source for history,[31] but because it is an integral part of the work as it now stands and was perhaps always an integral part of the work. The words of Zephaniah are meant to be read as though they had been

---

31. Haak, "Zephaniah's Oracles Against the Nations," raises the interesting question of whether prophetic writings can be used as historical sources.

spoken in the time of Josiah in the same sense that the events of the Book
of Ruth are meant to be understood as having taken place in the days of
the Judges.

What is true of the superscription is also true of other historical
references; their existence, even their accuracy, does not prove that the
date of composition is contemporaneous with the events portrayed. The
situation in Zephaniah is even more difficult, for outside of the superscription the book lacks references to specific historical events and
personages. But that has not deterred scholars from finding hints of them.
The best example is the prophecy against the nations in Chapter 2.
Because this prophecy mentions nations that existed during the seventh
century B.C.E. and were destroyed shortly thereafter (and also because of
the superscription), many biblicists conclude that this prophecy refers to
the situation in the time of Josiah and must therefore be a product of that
time. Now, while that is quite possible, it is by no means a foregone
conclusion. It is not certain, first of all, that a historical reference was
intended here; the list of nations may be just a formulaic listing of
traditional enemies. Or the prophecy may reflect post-Josianic events.
B. Peckham (14) interprets this prophecy as referring to the fall of
Nineveh, the battle of Carchemish in 605 B.C.E., and the Babylonian
campaigns against Philistia and Egypt in 604–601 B.C.E. But even
assuming that the prophecy against the nations does in fact allude to the
geopolitical situation between 640–612 (which is still a quite reasonable
view), we cannot conclude that the prophecy was written at that time.

Again, Ben Zvi's argument (298–306) addresses several salient points
in an interesting fashion. Among them are: (1) Philistia, Moab, and
Ammon are mentioned in other prophecies against the nations, and can
be considered formulaic enemies in this genre without reference to their
actual historical relationship to Judah. (2) The historical evidence that
Josiah conquered or attempted to control the territories of these nations
is absent or unconvincing, as is proof that he revolted against Assyria. (3)
Although references to the small nations in prophecies against the nations
may be formulaic, mention of the main power—Assyria, Babylonia, or
Egypt—is generally true to the historical setting. (4) The Bible in general
shows a good historical and geographical memory; people in the exilic
period would have known about the rise and fall of Assyria, the disposi-

tion of other countries, etc. (5) The purpose of this prophecy was to show that the words of Zephaniah regarding other nations had been fulfilled, and that therefore his words regarding the future of Judah in Chapter 3 would likewise be fulfilled. The choice of nations was made on the basis of those that had actually been destroyed between the time of Josiah and the time of the author of the prophecy. Assyria had indeed fallen, as had Philistia and the transjordanian kingdoms. Egypt is not mentioned because Egypt had not been conquered. Edom is absent because it was not conquered by Nebuchadnezzar but declined somewhat later, in the time of Nabonidus. Ben Zvi concludes that the prophecy against the nations best fits the situation of the early post-monarchic period, and he dates it to this time.

Another possibility is conceivable, although perhaps less likely than the others; namely, that the list of nations in this prophecy would have been most significant for a postexilic community seeking to carve out for itself a place at the junction of what had once been Philistia, Moab, Ammon, and the Assyrian province of Samerina (Samaria). Cf. Neh 13:1, 23, and other negative references to Ammonites, Moabites, Ashdodites, and various other enemies; and note that the indigenous population is called Canaanites in Neh 9:24.[32]

As the foregoing discussion shows, there are legitimate differences in interpretation of the historical, theological, and thematic aspects of Zephaniah as they relate to the dating of the book. The consensus is still that it was written during the time of Josiah. Ben Zvi's position is innovative, and it is too early to know what effect it will have on the consensus. But when one considers Zephaniah as part of the Twelve, instead of in isolation, the balance shifts toward Ben Zvi's position. Since the Twelve includes postexilic prophets, it cannot, as a whole and completed book, predate the postexilic period. This raises the question of how much of the Twelve was old material left undisturbed, how much was rewritten, and how much was written for the first time during the postexilic period.

---

32. Hoffman, *The Prophecies Against Foreign Nations in the Bible,* 179, suggests that additions to the original prophecy may have been made during the Restoration. Blenkinsopp, *The Pentateuch,* 87–89, hints that Genesis 9–10, to which I have linked Zephaniah 2, may have had input from the period of Ezra.

P. House, in *The Unity of the Twelve,* has argued for the structural, even narrative, integrity of the collection. House does not offer a date for individual books or for the Twelve, and does not present a detailed picture of how the individual books were shaped into the literary whole that he perceives; but implicit in his argument is the likelihood of a major reworking of the material of the minor prophets in order to forge them into a unified work. House's analysis seems forced and his conclusions about unity somewhat exaggerated, but he is not alone in seeing certain unifying aspects of the Twelve. F. I. Andersen and D. N. Freedman (*Hosea,* 57) says: "There is a sixth-century cast to the Book of the Twelve, and its function and objective are to be sought in a study of the needs and desires of the audience of that period." Here, too, is the idea that the individual books which had been written earlier were edited during the exile in conjunction with the formation of the Twelve, and perhaps edited again in the postexilic period.

Linguistic criteria present the same ambiguity as historical criteria. According to their orthography, all the books of the Twelve should be dated to the same time—the sixth century—owing to the influence of the process of compiling the Twelve. Yet no one would say that all twelve books were composed at the same time. Another promising avenue for linguistic dating is linguistic typology whereby the changes from classical biblical Hebrew to Late Biblical Hebrew (as in Ezra, Nehemiah, Chronicles) can be tracked. R. Polzin isolated the features of Late Biblical Hebrew in prose material. A. E. Hill applied Polzin's criteria to the postexilic prophets and found their date to be ca. 520–450 B.C.E. This type of analysis has not yet been done for Zephaniah. A. Hurvitz has developed linguistic criteria for recognizing late biblical psalms which might also be applicable to prophet works, although it is not clear if one can use the same criteria for dating different genres.[33] Moreover, linguistic dating does not yield absolute dates. It produces a relative chronology

---

33. One example of the type of problem that might arise has to do with the particle ʾt. Its absence or reduced frequency signals poetry, but Polzin found that in Late Biblical Hebrew prose there is an increased use of ʾt before a noun in the nominative case (for emphasis). Does Late Biblical Hebrew prophecy and poetry also manifest this increase, or does the tendency to eliminate the accusative particle ʾt also act to reduce this specialized use of ʾt?

based on statistical measures, that is, the likelihood in percentages that one text was written earlier than another. Nevertheless, more linguistic analysis of Zephaniah and other prophetic books would be useful.

The evidence for an absolute date for the composition of Zephaniah is inconclusive. However, the general parameters, which include most of the estimates based on historical and linguistic factors, are 630–520 B.C.E. This span, while perhaps not intolerably long in itself, contains a crucial historical moment, the exile in 586. And we will interpret the book's message quite differently depending on our estimate of which side of this divide it originated on. Perhaps the best way out of the dating dilemma is a compromise, not unlike that which is implicit or explicit in almost all discussions of prophetic books, including Ben Zvi's. That is to admit an earlier collection (perhaps from the time of Josiah), in unspecified form, of at least some prophet material (Ben Zvi's pre-compositional level), an exilic edition (Ben Zvi's compositional level), and perhaps a later, postexilic edition (Ben Zvi's post-compositional level). Whether we say the Book of Zephaniah was written during the late monarchy or during the post-monarchic period is, in the end, only a matter of where we put the emphasis. What do we mean by "written"? The first draft or the form recognizable as the canonical book? Whatever we decide, whether members of the exilic community composed the book or re-composed it, they are responsible for its existence, for without them the book would not be extant.

A postscript: The whole issue of dating, like textual criticism and other areas of biblical studies, is subject to changes over time. Much of the Bible was dated late by nineteenth-century scholars, then during the twentieth century dates were revised to reflect early oral traditions and even written traditions dating from the Davidic period. In several recent works the dates of many biblical books seem once again, although for different reasons, to be moving toward the exilic or postexilic period. For example, Peckham puts the Elohist at 650, after the Priestly Writer, and the Deuteronomist at 560. Blenkinsopp *(The Pentateuch)* views the Pentateuch as largely a product of the Persian period. It may be that Ben Zvi's later dating of Zephaniah is, unbeknownst to himself, part of a trend to give greater weight to texts in forms or editions closer to their canonical forms than to hypothetical proto-forms, and to accord more importance to the role of the exilic and postexilic Jewish community in the formation of the Bible.

The Historical Setting

The book is set in the time of Josiah. There are two questions that should be posed regarding the historical setting: (1) How does it compare with what modern historians know of this period? (2) How does it compare with the presentation of this period in other biblical texts? Finally, we should ask: If the book was written after the time of Josiah, how does the choice of this setting serve the purpose of the author or strengthen the message of the book?

Josiah reigned from 640 (or 639) to 609 B.C.E., a period of turmoil and change in the ancient near east; and a period for which our primary sources are few. Mesopotamian sources leave a gap between the last Assyrian document in 639 and the first entry in the Babylonian Chronicle in 626. Secondary sources add to the mystery and confusion: the Bible is silent on international events during the reign of Josiah (except for the notice of his death in an encounter with the Egyptian army), and Herodotus confuses us with his description of the Scythians and the siege of Ashdod (see Cazelles, Vaggione). Nevertheless, historians and archaeologists have been able to ascertain the general picture although there is disagreement on some of the details (see Haak, Na'aman, Oded, and Spalinger). The following is a brief summary as it pertains to the Book of Zephaniah.

The Assyrian empire had already incorporated the former northern kingdom of Israel into its territory, and had, at the height of its power, gained temporary control of Egypt. But when Josiah came to the throne, Assyria was entering a period of decline that would end in its destruction. For the first part of Josiah's reign, Ashurbanipal (668–627 B.C.E.) ruled Assyria and counted among his vassals Judah, Moab, Ammon, Edom, and the Philistine kingdoms. Troubles arose for the Assyrians in many directions: the growing power of Babylonia, a war with Elam, the movement of northern peoples—the Medes, Scythians, and Cimmerians—attacks by Arab tribes, and revolts of vassals. The position of Egypt, which was at times Assyria's ally and at other times its enemy, is not altogether clear. Egypt freed itself from Assyrian control in ca. 655 under the leadership of Psammetichus I. By the time that Neco II came to the throne in 610, Egypt had become a staunch Assyrian supporter against the greater threat of Babylonia. In the interim, Egypt had acquired control of the Mediterranean coast (Philistia), although whether this was accomplished by force or by peaceful agreement with the Assyrians is debated (see Haak, "Zephaniah's Oracles Against the Nations," and Na'aman).

The effect of these events on Judah must have been substantial, for the political changes in the world at large and as they affected Judah were quick and far-reaching. A mighty empire descended from its apogee, through a period of decline, to its death, during the reign of one Judean king, Josiah. Judah, nominally an independent kingdom, had been a vassal of this empire. One would naturally expect that the demise of its overlord and the rearrangement of the world's power structure had momentous import for Judah in terms of its internal political and religious policies, its alliances with foreign powers, and perhaps its territorial aspirations.

Yet the biblical sources present an incomplete picture, leaving it for historians to reconstruct almost everything except the religious tenor of the Josianic period. Although Josiah is the main focus of the "historical" texts, 2 Kings 22–23 and 2 Chronicles 34–35, they emphasize his religious activities, saying nothing about other internal policies or foreign powers except the account of Josiah's death by the hand of Pharaoh Neco. And because Kings and Chronicles had different agendas, they put the emphasis on different aspects of Josiah's reign. The prophets purporting to come from the Josianic period, Nahum, Zephaniah, and Jeremiah,[34] do seem to make references to the external situation but barely mention Josiah.

The Book of Kings portrays Josiah as a great religious reformer, equating him in some ways to Moses. Josiah is credited with removing all syncretistic practices from the cult—practices which, according to the

---

34. A few scholars date Habakkuk to this period, but most consider the mention of the Chaldeans as proof of a later date. See Roberts, 82–84.

Bible, had long been present and even supported by previous kings as early as Solomon, as well as some that may have been adopted more recently because of Assyrian influence. Scholars are agreed that the Assyrians did not formally impose their religion on their vassals (see Cogan), but it seems reasonable that many in Judah, especially in the ruling elite, would have found the practices of a wealthy and successful empire very attractive and would have promoted a degree of cultural and religious imitation if not assimilation. In addition, some Judean rulers might have sought to curry favor with the Assyrians through such cultural imitation. The result was syncretism—a layer of paganism superimposed on and intermingled with Israelite beliefs and practices. This was not a new phenomenon; it was an ever-present danger whenever there was contact between Israel and polytheistic countries, at least until the exile. But the contact and influence grew as Israel and Judah became players in an increasingly larger game of international relations.

Religious syncretism was the bane of the Deuteronomic and pro-phetic writings. It was for this sin that destruction would come to Israel and Judah. Kings like Hezekiah and Josiah who eradicated syncretism and instituted a return to purer, more authentically Israelite forms of worship are highly praised in the Bible. Thus, if a Deuteronomic writer wished to glorify a king, he would portray him exactly as 2 Kings has done. Na'aman ("The Kingdom of Judah under Josiah," 41, 55–59) observes that Kings was so eager to glorify Josiah that it altered the true picture by omitting much of the historical background, leaving the impression that Josiah was able to act independently of foreign dictates. In reality, as Na'aman sees it, Josiah was subordinate to foreign powers throughout his reign, first Assyria and then Egypt.

Chronicles, with its emphasis on Temple and cult, has made Josiah into a priest-king, more on the model of Samuel than Moses.[35] It makes the discovery of the scroll in the Temple secondary to the rebuilding of

---

35. The reference to Moses in 2 Kgs 23:25, and the phrase "before him there was no king like him . . . nor did any arise after him," reminiscent of the description of Moses in Deut 34:10, is lacking in Chronicles. Also, compare 2 Chr 35:18 and 2 Kgs 23:22: the Passover, which according to Kings had not been celebrated in like manner since the time of the Judges and kings, in Chronicles had not been celebrated thus since *Samuel* and the kings.

the Temple, and describes the Temple project and the Passover ritual extensively. It further enhances Josiah's reputation by having Jeremiah lament him. But, like Kings, on which it seems to have drawn, Chronicles omits all reference to external matters, except for the Neco incident, which is part of the main account instead of an epilogue as in 2 Kings.

Nahum's superscription offers no date. The book is a prophecy against Nineveh, which would, if we take it as historical, place it in the Assyrian period, before 612. The reference in 3:8 suggests that the *terminus a quo* is the fall of Thebes in 663. Roberts dates it to 640–630, which would put it in our period. But there is nothing that adds to the historical picture of this period or to the portrait of Josiah.

Jeremiah, according to the superscription, began his prophetic career in the thirteenth year of Josiah, 627 B.C.E., although there seems to have been a gap between his call and his first oracle five years later in 622. (This would have been the date, according to many, that Zephaniah's prophesying ended.) But, with the exception of 3:6, the dated prophecies are all from the reigns of later kings. Josiah is mentioned positively (22:15–16) but only for the purpose of comparison with his successor. While Jeremiah gives considerable space to foreign affairs, they are post-Josianic. The main threats are Babylonia and Egypt; Assyria is largely a has-been, noted for its destruction of the northern kingdom (e.g., 2:36). As for Judah's religious life, syncretism seems to have returned in full force.

The religious picture in Zephaniah 1 is similar to that which Josiah is said to have ameliorated in 2 Kings 23. But whether this refers to the pre- or post-Josianic situation (as does that in Jeremiah) can be debated. Unlike Jeremiah, both Zephaniah and Nahum give major billing to the destruction of Assyria, but whether that is to be taken as historical or symbolic is also debatable. (Note that Jonah also announces the destruction of Nineveh.)

None of the biblical sources presents enough information to reconstruct the history of the times. And because their genres and goals differ, it is inevitable that they would offer a slightly different picture of the same period. Kings and Chronicles focus on the king, while the prophets focus on foreign enemies and the religious corruption of Judah. Kings and Chronicles are "optimistic," giving the impression that Judah is secure and prospering under the leadership of the pious king Josiah. The prophets are by nature pessimistic, and picture Judah internally infirm and surrounded by hostile enemies. However, to the extent that Josiah is mentioned, he is mentioned positively in all the sources. And all the sources are unusually silent about the foreign policy of Josiah and specific events of the time. One may conclude that they have all idealized Josiah in slightly different ways.

Why was the period of Josiah chosen as the setting for Zephaniah? For those who date the book to this period, the question has no meaning; this is the period in which the prophet lived and spoke. His prophecy against Assyria and its vassals suggests that Zephaniah was among those urging Josiah to break away from Assyria and assert his independence. (Josiah apparently remained a loyal vassal.) Along with religious reform would come political independence—a rise in nationalism and a movement for autonomy that would have had a better chance of success now that Assyria was weakening and no other major power had yet filled the vacuum. Whether Zephaniah is actually advocating territorial expansion is a bone of contention. If so, expansion is to the east and west, not to Samaria in the north, as 2 Kings has it. Zephaniah's omission of Egypt may suggest that he was either pro-Egyptian or that he did not view Egypt as a threat.

For those who date the book later, the question is more acute. What did the Josianic period represent to a later generation? One guess is that it represented a small golden age, not quite like the time of David and Solomon but a time of religious and national aspirations under a pious and well-loved monarch. This is the internal view, the one in Kings and Chronicles. Complementing it is the external view offered by the prophets—a time of great international change, the fall of the first great empire, a new world order which offered hope (however short-lived) for Judah's improved position in the world. It was the best period, religiously and politically, between the division of the monarchy and the coming of Cyrus. An exilic or postexilic audience may have had a special affinity for a prophet speaking from this period, as it were, for they, too, held on to hopes of religious and national preservation or renewal, and knew the dangers of the rise and fall of empires.

BIBLIOGRAPHY

◆

Achtemeier, E. *Nahum-Malachi*. Interpretation. Atlanta: John Knox, 1986.

Ahlström, G. *Royal Administration and National Religion in Ancient Palestine*. Leiden: Brill, 1982.

Andersen, F. I. *The Sentence in Biblical Hebrew*. The Hague: Mouton, 1974.

Andersen, F. I., and Forbes, A. D. *The Computer Bible*. Vol. X. Biblical Research Associates, 1976.

Andersen, F. I., and Forbes, A. D. *Spelling in the Hebrew Bible*. Rome: Biblical Institute, 1986.

Andersen, F. I., and Freedman, D. N. *Amos*. AB. New York: Doubleday, 1989.

Anderson, F. I., and Freedman, D. N. *Hosea*. AB. New York: Doubleday, 1980.

Anderson, G. W. "The Idea of the Remnant in the Book of Zephaniah." *ASTI* 11 (1978): 11–14.

Avigad, N. *Discovering Jerusalem*. Nashville: T. Nelson, 1983.

———. *The Upper City of Jerusalem*. Jerusalem: Shikmona, 1980.

Bacher, W. "Zu Zephanja 2,4." ZAW 11 (1891): 185–87.

Baker, D. *Nahum, Habakkuk, Zephaniah*. Downers Grove, IL: Intervarsity, 1988.

Ball, I. J. "The Rhetorical Shape of Zephaniah." In *Perspectives on Language and Text*. Ed. E. W. Conrad and E. G. Newing. Winona Lake, IN: Eisenbrauns, 1987. Pp. 155–65.

———. *Zephaniah. A Rhetorical Study*. Berkeley: Bibal, 1988.

Bartlett, J. R. *Edom and the Edomites*. JSOT Suppl. 77. Sheffield: JSOT, 1989.

Begg, C. "The Non-mention of Zephaniah, Nahum and Habakkuk in the Deuteronomistic History," *BN* 38/39 (1987): 19–25.

Benoit, P., Milik, J. T., and de Vaux, R. *Les Grottes de Murabba'at*. *DJD* 1. Oxford: Clarendon, 1961.

Ben Zvi, E. *A Historical-Critical Study of the Book of Zephaniah*. BZAW vol. 198. Berlin: Walter de Gruyter, 1991.

Berlin, A. *The Dynamics of Biblical Parallelism*. Bloomington: Indiana University Press, 1985.

———. "Jeremiah 29:5–7: A Deuteronomic Allusion," *HAR* 8 (1984): 3–11.

Bewer, J. *The Book of the Twelve Prophets*. New York: Harper, 1949.

———. "Textual Suggestions on Isa 2:6; 66:3; Zeph 2:2,5." *JBL* 21 (1908): 163–66.

Blenkinsopp, J. *A History of Prophecy in Israel*. Philadelphia: Westminster, 1983.

———. *The Pentateuch*. The Anchor Bible Reference Library. New York: Doubleday, 1992.

Boadt, L. "Ezekiel, Book of." *ABD* II:711–22.

Bolle, M. *Seper Ṣepanya*. In *Tere ʿaśar ʿim peruš daʿat miqraʾ*, Vol II. Jerusalem: Mosad Harav Kook, 1970.

Bracke, J. M. "Šub šebut: A Reappraisal." *ZAW* 97 (1985): 233–44.

Brensinger, T. L. *Lions, Wind and Fire: A Study of Prophetic Similes*. Dissert. Drew University. Madison, NJ, 1985.

Brin, G. "On the title *bn hmlk*." *Lešonenu* 31 (1967): 5–20, 85–96.

———. "The Title *ben (ham-)melek*, and Its Parallels: The Significance and Evaluation of an Official Title." *AION* 29 (1969): 432–65.

Broshi, M. "Estimating the Population of Ancient Jerusalem." *BAR* 4 (1978): 10–15.

———. "La population de l'ancienne Jerusalem." *RB* 82 (1975): 5–14.

Brown, R. E., Fitzmyer, J. A., and Murphy, R. E. (eds.). *The New Jerome Biblical Commentary*. Englewood Cliffs: Prentice-Hall, 1990.

Cahana, A. *Seper Tere ʿAśar*. Tel Aviv: Meqorot, 1930.

Cathcart, K. J. "*bošet* in Zephaniah 3:5." *JNSL* 12 (1984): 35–39.

———. "Day of Yahweh." *ABD* II:84–85.

Cathcart, K. J., and Gordon, R. P. *The Targum of the Minor Prophets.* Wilmington: Michael Glazier, 1989.

Cazelles, H. "Sophonie, Jeremie at les Scythes en Palastine," *RB* 74 (1964): 24–44.

———. "Zephaniah, Jeremiah, and the Scythians in Palestine." In *A Prophet to the Nations: Essays in Jeremiah Studies.* Ed. Leo Perdue and Brian W. Kovacs. Winona Lake, IN: Eisenbrauns, 1984. Pp. 129–49.

Christensen, D. "Zephaniah 2:4–15: A Theological Basis for Josiah's Program of Political Expansion." *CBQ* 46 (1984): 669–82.

Claburn, W. E. "The Fiscal Basis of Josiah's Reforms." *JBL* 92 (1973): 11–22.

Clark, D. J. "Of Birds and Beasts: Zephaniah 2.14." *BT* 34 (1983): 243–46.

———. "Wine on the Lees (Zeph 1.12 & Jer 48.11)." *BT* 32 (1981): 241–43.

Clark, D. J., and Hatton, H. A. *Translator's Handbook on the Books of Nahum, Habakkuk, and Zephaniah.* American Bible Society.

Clifford, R. J. "The Use of *Hoy* in the Prophets." *CBQ* 28 (1966): 458–64.

Cogan, M. *Imperialism and Religion: Assyria, Judah, and Israel in the Eighth and Seventh Centuries B.C.E.* Missoula, MT: Scholars, 1974.

Davidson, A. B. *The Books of Nahum, Habakkuk and Zephaniah.* Cambridge: Cambridge University Press, 1899.

Day, J. *Molech: A God of Human Sacrifice in the Old Testament.* Cambridge: Cambridge University Press, 1989.

Delcor, M. "Les Kerethim et les Cretois." *VT* 28 (1978): 409–22.

De Roche, M. "Zephaniah 1:2–3: The 'Sweeping' of Creation." *VT* 30 (1980): 104–9.

De Vaux, R. *Ancient Israel.* New York: McGraw-Hill, 1965.

Diessler, A. *Zwölf Propheten III: Zephanja, Haggai, Sacharja, Maleachi.* Würzburg: Echter, 1988.

Donner, H. "Die Schwellenhupfer: Beobachtungen zu Zephanja 1,8f." *JSS* 15 (1970): 42–55.

Eaton, J. H. *Obadiah, Nahum, Habakkuk, and Zephaniah.* London: SCM, 1961.

Edler, R. *Das Kerygma des Propheten Zefanja*. Freiburg, 1984.

Efros, I. "Textual Notes on the Hebrew Bible." *JAOS* 45 (1925): 152–54.

Ehrlich, A. B. *Mikra ki-pheshuto*. Vol. III. New York: Ktav, 1969 (first pub. 1901).

Elat, M. "The Political Status of the Kingdom of Judah within the Assyrian Empire in the 7th Century B.C.E." In *Investigations at Lachish: The Sanctuary and the Residency (Lachish V)*. Ed. Y. Aharoni et al. Tel Aviv: Gateway, 1975. Pp. 61–70.

Elliger, K. *Das Buch der zwölf Kleinen Propheten, II. Die Propheten Nahum, Habakkuk, Zephanja, Haggai, Sacharja, Maleachi*. Göttingen: Vandenhoeck & Ruprecht, 1967.

———. "Das Ende der 'Abendwölfe' Zeph 3,3 Hab 1,8." In *Festschrift für Alfred Bertholet zum 80. Geburtstag*. Ed. W. Baumgartner et al. Tübingen: J. C. B. Mohr, 1950. Pp. 158–75.

Eph'al, I. *The Ancient Arabs*. Jerusalem and Leiden: Magnes and Brill, 1982.

Eszenyei Szeles, M. E. *Wrath and Mercy: A Commentary on the Books of Habakkuk and Zephaniah*. Grand Rapids: Eerdmans, 1987.

Everson, A. J. "Day of the Lord." *IDBSup*. 209–10.

———. "The Days of Yahweh," *JBL* 93 (1974): 329–37.

Fensham, F. C. "The Poetic Form of the Hymn of the Lord in Zephanjah." *Die Ou Testamentiese Werkgemeenskap Suid-Afrika* 13/14 (1970/71): 9–14.

———. "A Possible Origin of the Concept of the Day of the Lord." *Die Ou Testamentiese Werkgemeenskap Suid-Afrika* 10 (1967): 90–97.

———. "Zephaniah, Book of." *IDBSup*. 983–84.

Ferguson, H. "The Historical Testimony of the Prophet Zephaniah." *JBL* 3 (1883): 42–59.

Fowler, J. D. *Theophoric Personal Names in Ancient Hebrew: A Comparative Study*. JSOT Suppl. 49. Sheffield: JSOT, 1988.

Fox, M. V. *The Redaction of the Books of Esther*. Atlanta: Scholars, 1991.

Gaster, T. "Two Textual Emendations—Zephaniah iii 17." *ET* 78 (1966–67): 267.

Geller, S. A. "Cleft Sentences with Pleonastic Pronoun: A Syntactic Construction of Biblical Hebrew and Some of Its Literary Uses." *Journal of the Ancient Near Eastern Society* 20 (1991): 15–33.

Gelston, A. *The Old Testament in Syriac. According to the Peshitta. Dodekapropheton*. Leiden: Brill, 1980.

———. *The Peshitta of the Twelve Prophets*. Oxford: Clarendon, 1987.

Gerleman, G. *Zephanja: Textkritisch und Literarisch Untersucht*. Lund: C. W. K. Gleerup, 1942.

Gerstenberger, E. "The Woe-oracles of the Prophets." *JBL* 81 (1962): 249–63.

Geyer, J. B. "Mythology and Culture in the Oracles Against the Nations." *VT* 36 (1986): 129–45.

Ginsberg, H. L. "Judah and the Transjordan States from 734 to 582 B.C.E." In *Alexander Marx Jubilee Volume*. New York: Jewish Theological Seminary of America, 1950. Pp. 337–68.

———. "Some Emendations in Isaiah." *JBL* 69 (1950): 51–60.

Glazier McDonald, B. "Review of P. House, *Zephaniah*." *JBL* 108 (1990): 517–19.

Gordis, R. "A Rising Tide of Misery: A Note on a Note on Zephaniah II, 4." *VT* 37 (1987): 487–90.

Gray, J. "A Metaphor from Building in Zephaniah II 1." *VT* 3 (1953): 404–7.

Greenberg, M. *Ezekiel 1–20*. AB. Garden City, NY: Doubleday, 1983.

Greenfield, J. C. "A Hapax Legomenon, *mimšaq ḥarul*." In *Studies in Judaica, Karaitica, and Islamica Presented to Leon Nemoy on His 80th Birthday*. Ed. S. Brunswick. Ramat Gan: Bar Ilan University Press, 1982. Pp. 79–85.

Grill, F. "Der Schlachttag Jahwes." *BZ* 2 (1958): 278–83.

Gruber, M. *Aspects of Non-Verbal Communication in the Ancient Near East*. Rome: Biblical Institute, 1980.

———. "Fear, Anxiety and Reverence in Akkadian, Biblical Hebrew and Other North-West Semitic Languages," *VT* 40 (1990): 411–22.

Haak, R. D. *Habakkuk*. VTS 44. Leiden: Brill, 1992.

———. "Zephaniah's Oracles Against the Nations." Unpublished paper read at the Chicago Society of Biblical Research, 2 February 1992.

Hamborg, G. R. "Reasons for Judgment in the Oracles against the Nations of the Prophet Isaiah." *VT* 31 (1981): 145–59.

Haupt, P. "Pelican and Bittern." *JBL* 39 (1920): 158–61.

———. "Qaš, straw, and qäšt, bow." *JBL* 39 (1920): 160–63.

Hayes, J. H. "The Usage of Oracles Against Foreign Nations in Ancient Israel." *JBL* 87 (1968): 81–92.

Heflin, J. N. *Nahum, Habakkuk, Zephaniah, and Haggai.* Grand Rapids: Lamplighter, 1985.

Heider, G. C. *The Cult of Molek.* JSOT Suppl. 43. Sheffield: JSOT, 1985.

Heintz, J. G. "Aux origines d'une expression biblique: ūmušu qerbū." *VT* 21 (1971): 528–40.

Heller, J. "Zephanjas Ahnenreihe," *VT* 21 (1971): 102–4.

Hestrin, R., et al., eds. *Inscriptions Reveal. Documents from the Time of the Bible, the Mishnah and the Talmud.* Jerusalem: Israel Museum, 1973.

Hiebert, T. "House's *Zephaniah*: A Prophetic Drama," *JQR* 81 (1990): 175–78.

Hiers, R. "Day of the Lord." *ABD* II:82–83. New York: Doubleday, 1992.

Hill, A. E. "Dating the Book of Malachi: A Linguistic Reexamination." In *The Word of the Lord Shall Go Forth.* Ed. C. L. Meyers and M. O'Connor. Winona Lake, IN: Eisenbrauns, 1983. Pp. 77–89.

Hillers, D. "Dust: Some Aspects of Old Testament Imagery." In *Love and Death in the Ancient Near East. Essays in Honor of Marvin H. Pope.* Ed. J. H. Marks and R. M. Good. Guilford, CT: Four Quarters, 1987. Pp. 105–9.

———. "*Hoy* and *Hoy*-Oracles: A Neglected Syntactic Aspect." In *The Word of the Lord Shall Go Forth.* Ed. C. Meyers and M. O'Connor. Winona Lake, IN: Eisenbrauns, 1983. Pp. 185–88.

Hoffman, Y. "The Day of the Lord as a Concept and a Term in the Prophetic Literature." *ZAW* 93 (1981): 37–50.

———. "From Oracle to Prophecy: The Growth, Crystallization, and Disintegration of a Biblical Gattung," *JNSL* 10 (1982): 75–81.

———. *The Prophecies Against Foreign Nations in the Bible.* Tel Aviv: Tel Aviv University Press, 1977 [Hebrew].

Horgan, M. P. *Pesharim: Qumran Interpretations of Biblical Books. CBQ Monograph Series* 8. Washington, DC: Catholic Biblical Association of America, 1979.

House, P. R. *The Unity of the Twelve.* Bible and Literature Series 27. Sheffield: Almond, 1990.

———. *Zephaniah. A Prophetic Drama.* Bible and Literature Series 16. Sheffield: Almond, 1988.

Humbert, P. " 'Etendre la main' (Note de lexicographie hébraïque)." *VT* 12 (1962): 383–95.

Hunter, A. V. *Seek the Lord! A Study of the Meaning and Function of the Exhortation in Amos, Hosea, Isaiah, Micah, and Zephaniah.* Baltimore: St. Mary's Seminary, 1982.

Hurvitz, A. *Ben Lašon Lelašon.* Jerusalem: Mosad Bialik, 1972.

Hyatt, J. P. "The Date and Background of Zephaniah." *JNES* 7 (1948): 25–29.

———. "The Peril From the North in Jeremiah." *JBL* 59 (1940): 449–513.

Ibn Caspi, Joseph. *ʾAdnê Keseph.* Part II. Ed. Isaac Last. London: Y. Groditsky, 1911–12.

Ihromi. *ʿAmm ʿAni Wadal nach dem Propheten Zephanja.* Mainz: Johannes Gutenberg Universität, 1972.

———. "Die Haufung der Verben des Jubelns in Zephaniah III 14f, 16–18: *rnn, rwᶜ, śmḥ, ᶜlz, śwś* und *gil.*" *VT* 33 (1983): 106–10.

Irsigler, H. "Äquivalenz in Poesie: Die kontextuellen Synonyme *ṣaᶜaqa - yalala - šibr gadu(w)l* in Zef 1, 10 c. d. e." *BZ* 22 (1978): 221–35.

———. *Gottesgericht und Jahwetag: Die Komposition Zef 1,1–2,3, untersucht auf der Grundlage der Literarkritik des Zefanjabuches.* St. Ottilien: EOS Verlag, 1977.

Jeppesen, K. "Zephaniah I 5B." *VT* 31 (1981): 372–73.

Jongeling, B. "Jeux de mots en Sophonie III 1 et 3?" *VT* 21 (1971): 541–47.

Kapelrud, A. S. "Eschatology in Micah and Zephaniah." In *De la Torah au Messie, Études d'exégèse et d'herméneutique bibliques offertes à Henri CAZELLES pour ses 25 années d'enseignement à l'Institut Catholique de Paris (Octobre 1979).* Ed. M. Carrez et al. Paris: Desclée de Brouwer, 1981. Pp. 255–62.

———. *The Message of the Prophet Zephaniah: Morphology and Ideas.* Oslo: Universitetsforlaget, 1975.

King, G. A. "Recent Trends in the Study of Zephaniah." Paper read at

Annual Meeting of Society of Biblical Literature, San Francisco, 1992.

Koch, K. *The Prophets*. Vol. I. *The Assyrian Period*. Philadelphia: Fortress, 1983.

Kraeling, E. G. *Commentary on the Prophets*. Vol. II. *Daniel–Malachi*. Camden, NJ: Thomas Nelson & Sons, 1966.

Krinetzki, G. *Zefanjastudien: Motiv- und Traditionskritik + Kompositions- und Redaktionskritik*. Frankfort: Peter Lang, 1977.

Kselman, J. S. "A Note on Jer 49,20 and Ze 2,6–7." *CBQ* 32 (1970): 579–81.

———. "Zephaniah, Book of." *ABD* VI:1077–80.

Kutler, L. "A 'Strong' Case for the Hebrew 'MAR.' " *UF* 16 (1984): 111–18.

Langohr, G. "Le livre Sophonie et la critique d'authenticité." *Ephemerides Theologicae Lovanienses* 52 (1976): 1–27.

———. "Redaction et composition du livre de Sophonie," *Le Muséon* 89 (1976): 51–73.

Lemaire, A. "Note sur le titre 'BN HMLK' dans l'Ancient Israël." *Semitica* 29 (1979): 59–65.

Leslie, E. A. "Zephaniah, Book of." *IDB: R–Z*. Nashville: Abingdon, 1962, 951–53.

Levenson, J. D. *Creation and the Persistence of Evil*. San Francisco: Harper and Row, 1988.

Lloyd, S. *The Archaeology of Mesopotamia*. London: Thames and Hudson, 1984.

Lohfink, N. "Zephanja und das Israel der Armen." *BK* 39 (1984): 100–8.

Loretz, O. "Textologie des Zephanja-Buches." *UF* 5 (1973): 219–28.

Machinist, P. "Assyria and Its Image in the First Isaiah." *JAOS* 103 (1983): 719–37.

Malamat, A. "The Historical Setting of Two Biblical Prophecies on the Nations," *IEJ* 1 (1950): 154–59.

Malbim (Meir Leibush ben Yeḥiel Michael). *ʾOṣar haperushim ʿal tanakh . . . perush hamalbim*. Jerusalem: Pardes, 1956.

Mandelkern, S. *Concordantiae Hebraicae atque Chaldaicae*. Jerusalem and Tel Aviv: Schocken, 1962.

Margolis, M. "Zephaniah." In A. Cahana, *Seper Tere ʿAśar.*

Marti, D. K. *Das Dodekapropheton.* Tübingen: J. C. B. Mohr, 1904.

Martin, F. "Le livre de Sophonie." *Semiotique et Bible* 39 (1985): 1–22; 40 (1986): 5–20.

Mazar, B. *Encyclopedia of Archaeological Excavations in the Holy Land.* Jerusalem: Hebra lehaqirat ʾereṣ yisraʾel weʿatiqoteha, 1970.

McCarter, P. K. *Textual Criticism.* Philadelphia: Fortress, 1986.

Mendecki, N. "Koniec Utrapien—Wywyzszenie Izraela u Sof 3, 18–20 [German abstract: "Das Ende der Schmach und die Erhohung Israels in Zef 3, 18–20."]. *Collectanea Theologica* 53/4 (1983): 53–59.

Milgrom, J. *Numbers.* The JPS Torah Commentary. Philadelphia: Jewish Publication Society, 1990.

Millard, A. R. "The Scythian Problem." In *Glimpses of Ancient Egypt.* Ed. J. Ruffle, G. A. Gaballa, and K. A. Kitchen. Warminster: Aris and Phillips, 1979. Pp. 119–22.

Miqraʾot Gedolot (Rabbinic Bible). Tel Aviv: Pardes, 1958–59.

Muraoka, T. *Emphatic Words and Structures in Biblical Hebrew.* Jerusalem and Leiden: Magnes and Brill, 1985.

Naʾaman, N. "Chronology and History in the Late Assyrian Empire (631–619 B.C.)." ZA 81 (1991): 243–67.

———. "The Kingdom of Judah under Josiah." *Tel Aviv* 18 (1991): 3–71.

Nel, P. J. "Structural and Conceptual Strategy in Zephaniah, Chapter 1." *JNSL* 15 (1989): 155–67.

O'Connor, M. *Hebrew Verse Structure.* Winona Lake, IN: Eisenbrauns, 1980.

Oded, B. "Judah and the Exile." In *Israelite and Judean History.* Ed. J. H. Hayes and J. M. Miller. Philadelphia: Westminster, 1977. Pp. 435–88.

———. "Neighbors in the East." In *The World History of the Jewish People Vol. IV. The Age of Monarchies: 1, Political History.* Ed. A. Malamat and I. Eph'al. Jerusalem: Jewish History Publications and Massada Press, 1979. Pp. 247–75.

———. "Observations on Methods of Assyrian Rule in Transjordania after the Palestinian Campaign of Tiglath-Pileser III." *JNES* 29 (1970): 177–86.

————. "The Table of Nations (Genesis 10)—A Socio-cultural Approach." ZAW 98 (1986): 14–31.

Oeming, M. "Gericht Gottes und Geschicke der Völker nach Zef 3, 1–13." TQ 167 (1987): 289–300.

Olivier, J. P. J. "A Possible Interpretation of the Word ṣiyya in Zeph 2,13." JNSL 8 (1980): 95–97.

Patterson, R. D. Nahum, Habakkuk, Zephaniah. The Wycliffe Exegetical Commentary. Chicago: Moody, 1991.

Paul, S. M. Amos. Hermeneia. Minneapolis: Fortress, 1991.

Peckham, B. History and Prophecy. The Development of Late Judean Literary Traditions. The Anchor Bible Reference Library. New York: Doubleday, 1993.

Petersen, D. "The Oracles Against the Nations: A Form-critical Analysis." SBL Seminar Papers, 1975, I 39–46.

Polzin, R. Late Biblical Hebrew. Towards an Historical Typology of Biblical Hebrew Prose. Missoula: Scholars, 1976.

Rice, G. "The African Roots of the Prophet Zephaniah." Journal of Religious Thought 36 (1979): 21–31.

Rice, T. T. The Scythians. London: Thames and Hudson, 1957.

Rimbach, J. A. "Those Lively Prophets—Zephaniah Ben-Cushi." Currents in Theology and Mission 7 (1980): 239–42.

Roberts, J. J. M. Nahum, Habakkuk and Zephaniah. Old Testament Library. Philadelphia: Westminster, 1991.

Robertson, O. P. The Books of Nahum, Habakkuk, and Zephaniah. The New International Commentary on the Old Testament. Grand Rapids: Eerdmans, 1990.

Rosenberg, J. "Jeremiah and Ezekiel" in The Literary Guide to the Bible. Ed. R. Alter and F. Kermode. Cambridge, MA: Belknap, 1987. Pp. 184–206.

Rudolph, W. Micha—Nahum—Habakkuk—Zephanja. Kommentar zum Alten Testament. Bd. XIII/3. Gutersloh: Gutersloher Verlagshaus Gerd Mohn, 1975.

Sabottka, L. Zephanja: versuch einer Neuübersetzung mit philologischem Kommentar. Biblica et Orientala 25. Rome: Biblical Institute Press, 1972.

Sarna, N. M. "Bible," Encyclopedia Judaica 4: 814–36.

Sasson, J. M. *Jonah*. AB. New York: Doubleday, 1990.

Sauer, J. A. "Ammon, Moab and Edom." In *Biblical Archaeology Today*. Ed. J. Amitai. Jerusalem: Israel Exploration Society, 1985. Pp. 206–14.

Scharbert, J. "Zefanja und die Reform des Joschija." In *Künder des Wortes: Beiträge zur Theologie der Propheten, J. Schreiner zum 60. Geburtstag*. Ed. L. Ruppert et al. Würzburg: Echter, 1982. Pp. 237–53.

Schiffman, L. H. "Review of *The Greek Minor Prophets Scroll from Nahal Hever*". *JBL* 111 (1992): 532–35.

Schoville, K. N. "A Note on the Oracles of Amos Against Gaza, Tyre, and Edom." *VTS* 26 (1974): 55–63.

Segal, M. Z. *Šenem ʿAśar*. Tel Aviv: Dvir, 1947.

Sellin, E. *Das Zwölfprophetenbuch*. Leipzig: A. Deichert, 1930.

Seybold, K. *Nahum, Habakuk Zephanja*. Züricher Bibelkommentare. Zürich: Theologische Verlag, 1991.

———. *Satirische Prophetie: Studien zum Buch Zefanja*. Stuttgarter Bibelstudien 120. Stuttgart: Katholisches Bibelwerk, 1985.

———. "Text und Textauslegung in Zef 2, 1–3." *Biblische Notizen* 25 (1984): 49–54.

———. "Die Verwendung der Bildmotive in der Prohetie Zefanjas." In *Beiträge zur prophetischen Bildsprachen in Israel und Assyrien*. Ed. H. Weippert et al. Freiburg: Universitätsverlag; Göttingen: Vandenhoeck & Ruprecht, 1985. Pp. 30–45.

Smith, G. A. *The Book of the Twelve Prophets Commonly Called the Minor*, Vol II. The Expositor's Bible. New York: Armstrong, 1898.

Smith, J. M. P., Ward, W. H., and Bewer, J. A. *Micah, Zephaniah, Nahum, Habakkuk, Obadiah, and Joel*. ICC. Edinburgh: T. and T. Clark, 1911.

Smith, L., and Lacheman, E. R. "The Authorship of the Book of Zephaniah." *JNES* 9 (1950): 137–42.

Smith, R. L. *Micah-Malachi*. Word Bible Commentary. Waco: Word, 1984.

Spalinger, A. "Assurbanipal and Egypt: A Source Study," *JAOS* 94 (1974): 316–28.

———. "The Concept of Monarchy During the Saite Epoch—an Essay of Synthesis," *Orientalia* 47 (1978): 12–36.

————. "The Date of the Death of Gyges and Its Historical Implications," *JAOS* 98 (1978): 400–9.

————. "Psammetichus, King of Egypt: I," *JARCE* 13 (1976): 133–47.

————. "Psammetichus, King of Egypt: II," *JARCE* 15 (1978): 49–57.

Speiser, E. A. *Genesis.* AB. Garden City, NY: Doubleday, 1964.

————. "The Rivers of Paradise." In *Oriental and Biblical Studies.* Ed. J. J. Finkelstein and M. Greenberg. Philadelphia: University of Pennsylvania Press, 1967, 23–34.

Stenzel, M. "Zum Verständnis von Zephanja III 3b." *VT* 1 (1951): 303–5.

Sweeney, M. A. "A Form-Critical Reassessment of the Book of Zephaniah." *CBQ* 53 (1991): 388–408.

Tadmor, H. "Philistia under Assyrian Rule." *BA* 29 (1966): 86–102.

Tadmor, H. and Cogan, M. *2 Kings.* AB. Garden City, NY: Doubleday, 1988.

Tatford, F. A. *Prophet of Royal Blood; an Exposition of the Prophecy of Zephaniah.* Eastbourne, Sussex, 1973.

Taylor, C. L. "Zephaniah." *Interpreter's Bible.* Ed. G. A. Buttrick et al. Nashville: Abingdon, 1956. Pp. 1007–34.

Thomas, D. W. "A Pun on the Name of Ashdod in Zephaniah ii.4." *ET* 74 (1962–63): 63.

Thompson, J. A. "The 'Response' in Biblical and Non-Biblical Literature with Particular Reference to the Hebrew Prophets." In *Perspectives on Language and Text.* Ed. E. W. Conrad and E. G. Newing. Winona Lake, IN: Eisenbrauns, 1987. Pp. 255–68.

Tigay, J. H. *You Shall Have No Other Gods: Israelite Religion in the Light of Hebrew Inscriptions.* Atlanta: Scholars, 1986.

Tov, E. *The Greek Minor Prophets Scroll from Naḥal Ḥever.* DJD 8. Oxford: Clarendon, 1990.

————. *Textual Criticism of the Hebrew Bible.* Minneapolis: Fortress, 1992.

Tsevat, M. "Some Biblical Notes—(Zeph 3.17ff)." *HUCA* 24 (1952–53): 107–14.

Tushingham, A. D. "The Western Hill under the Monarchy." *ZDPV* 95 (1975): 39–55.

Vaggione, R. P. "Over All Asia? The Extent of the Scythian Domination in Herodotus." *JBL* 92 (1973): 523–30.

van Grol, H. W. M. "Classical Hebrew Metrics and Zeph. 2–3." In *The Structural Analysis of Biblical and Canaanite Poetry*. Ed. W. van der Meer and J. C. de Moor. JSOT Supplement Series 74. Sheffield: JSOT, 1988. Pp. 186–206.

van Zyl, A. H. *The Moabites*. Leiden: Brill, 1960.

von Rad, G. "The Origin of the Concept 'Day of Yahweh.' " *JSS* 4 (1959): 97–108.

Waltke, B., and O'Connor, M. *An Introduction to Biblical Hebrew Syntax*. Winona Lake, IN: Eisenbrauns, 1990.

Watts, J. D. *The Books of Joel, Obadiah, Jonah, Nahum, Habakkuk, and Zephaniah*. Cambridge: Cambridge University Press, 1975.

Weinfeld, M. *Deuteronomy 1–11*. AB. New York: Doubleday, 1991.

———. *Deuteronomy and the Deuteronomic School*. Oxford: Clarendon, 1972.

———. "The Worship of Molech and the Queen of Heaven and Its Background." *UF* 4 (1972): 133–54.

Weingreen, J. *An Introduction to the Critical Study of the Text of the Hebrew Bible*. Oxford: Clarendon, 1982.

Weiss, M. *The Bible from Within*. Jerusalem: Magnes, 1984.

———. "The Origin of the 'Day of the Lord' Reconsidered." *HUCA* 38 (1966): 29–63.

Wellhausen. J. *Die kleinen Propheten: übersetzt und erklärt*. Vierte unveränderte Auflage. Berlin: Walter de Gruyter, 1963.

Wiklander, B. *Prophecy as Literature. A Text-Linguistic and Rhetorical Approach to Isaiah 2–4*. Coniectanea Biblica. Old Testament Series 22. Uppsala: C. W. K. Gleerup, 1984.

Williams, D. "The Date of Zephaniah." *JBL* 82 (1963): 77–88.

Wilson, R. R. *Genealogy and History in the Biblical World*. New Haven: Yale University Press, 1977.

———. *Prophecy and Society in Ancient Israel*. Philadelphia: Fortress, 1980.

Wintermute, O. S. "The Apocalypse of Zephaniah." In *The Old Testament Pseudepigrapha*. Ed. J. H. Charlesworth. Vol. I. Garden City, NY: Doubleday, 1983. Pp. 497–515.

Würthwein, E. *The Text of the Old Testament*. Grand Rapids: Eerdmans, 1979.

Yamauchi, E. "The Scythians: Invading Hordes from the Russian Steppes," *BA* 46 (1983): 90–97.

Zalcman, L. "Ambiguity and Assonance at Zephaniah ii 4." *VT* 36 (1986): 365–71.

———. "*Di Sera*, Desert, Dessert." *ET* 91 (1979): 311.

Zandstra, S. *The Witness of the Vulgate, Peshitta and Septuagint to the Text of Zephaniah*. New York: Columbia University Press, 1909.

NOTES
AND
COMMENTS

♦

I. SUPERSCRIPTION (1:1)

♦

1:1 The word of the Lord which came to Zephaniah son of Cushi son of Gedaliah son of Amariah son of Hezekiah in the days of Josiah son of Amon, king of Judah.

NOTES

1:1. *The word of the Lord which came to.* Similar superscriptions stand at the beginning of Hosea, Micah, and Joel. See also Jer 1:2 and Zech 1:1, and the slightly different Hag 1:1. This construction, putting "the word" at the head of the verse, is a standard way of introducing a prophetic message and puts the emphasis on the contents of the message, rather than on the person of the prophet.

For an extensive discussion of prophetic superscriptions, see Andersen and Freedman, *Hosea*, 143–49. They stress the similarities among the eighth-century prophets (Amos, Hosea, Isaiah, and Micah) and the differences between these and the seventh-century prophets (Jeremiah and Zephaniah), concluding that the books of the eighth-century prophets could not have been edited in the late seventh or early sixth century, for then their superscriptions would be more similar to the seventh-century prophetic superscriptions. These superscriptions must, therefore, have been supplied close to the time that the prophet lived. Presumably Andersen and Freedman would say the same for the seventh- and sixth-century prophetic books. We will note, however, that there are some indications that the superscription of Zephaniah is postexilic.

The word of the Lord. This phrase is a technical term for prophecy or prophetic oracle. Of the close to 250 times it occurs in the Hebrew Bible, the overwhelming majority are in connection with prophets. *Dabar,* "word," is specifically associated with the prophet in Jer 18:18. The grammatical singular may be understood as a collective. The plural is used much less frequently in connection with prophets and in a different sense: "matters, story"—cf. Andersen and Freedman, *Amos,* 184.

Wilson (*Prophecy and Society in Ancient Israel,* 145) associates the formula "the word of the Lord" with the notion of possession by God in the Ephraimite tradition and with a few pre-exilic (Judean) prophetic texts. Other scholars have associated the term with deuteronomistic popularization. I agree with Sasson (*Jonah,* 68), however, that the term "word of the Lord" is such a commonplace that it is not helpful to assign it to a specific period or group. For a complete discussion on the usages of *dabar* see *TDOT* III, 103–25.

Ben Zvi, 42, states that the text that follows "the word of the Lord" need not consist of the actual words spoken by God to the prophet. Hence he takes *dabar* in its broader sense, "matter."

Which came to. The syntax (with a noun, "the word of the Lord," at the head of the clause) does not seem to emphasize the process of communication to the prophet as much as to specify ownership of the oracle to follow: this is Zephaniah's oracle, the Lord's word to Zephaniah, as opposed to the oracle of another prophet.

Zephaniah. The name means "YHWH has hidden, protected, treasured" (cf. Ps 31:20–21). Its form is a common one: *Qal* perfect plus theophoric element, and is echoed in two others in the genealogy, Gedaliah and Amariah. The root *ṣpn* occurs in other biblical names; cf. Elzaphan and Elizaphan (Exod 6:22; Lev 10:4; Num 3:30; 34:25; 1 Chr 15:8; 2 Chr 29:13). For extrabiblical names with the element *ṣpn* see Fowler, *Theophoric Personal Names in Ancient Israel: A Comparative*

Study, 105, 358. The name *ṣpnyhw* appears on a seal impression from early sixth-century Lachish (Hestrin, 25).

The same name is borne by a priest in the time of Jeremiah (Jer 21:1; 29:25, 29; 37:3; 52:24; 2 Kgs 25:18). A third Zephaniah is mentioned in Zech 6:10, 14, and a fourth in 1 Chr 6:21.

Son of Cushi . . . Hezekiah. This prophetic genealogy, containing four preceding generations, is unusually long. For a discussion of other genealogies going back four or more generations see Ben Zvi, 42–43. Medieval Jewish commentaries and some modern scholars have suggested that it reached back until it came to a famous ancestor, Hezekiah, whom some identified with the king of Judah (so Ibn Ezra; J. M. P. Smith, ICC, also accepts this identification). Others (e.g., Kimḥi) questioned whether Hezekiah here was indeed the king, but felt, nevertheless, that the list must contain the names of important people whose appearance here would lend greater prestige to Zephaniah.

Robert Wilson (*Prophecy and Society in Ancient Israel*, 279–80) observes that since the genealogy is abnormally long, it must have served a specific purpose. He notes that linear genealogies of this type serve only one function: to ground in the past the individual's claim to power or position. The most important name in such a genealogy is the earliest, the ancestor from whom the prestige is ultimately inherited—in this case Hezekiah. Therefore, it makes much more sense to view this Hezekiah as the former king of Judah, rather than an otherwise unknown Hezekiah.

The link with Hezekiah not only has implications about the family status of Zephaniah, but may also suggest a connection with Hezekiah's religious reforms, which were not unlike those of Josiah. The superscription hints that Zephaniah's apparent support of religious reform in his own day has an origin in his family history. He was not a newcomer to the reform movement and was, perhaps, among those urging it even before Josiah instituted it. As a descendant of Hezekiah, Zephaniah would also be a relative of Josiah and hence a member of the ruling elite (private communication, DNF).

The Peshitta and a few masoretic manuscripts (see J. M. P. Smith et al., 185) read "Hilkiah." This is the name of the high priest under Josiah but could not refer to the same person. A second Hilkiah is the father of Eliakim, overseer of the household of Hezekiah (2 Kgs 18:37 and passim). If this is the person meant, then it, too, puts Zephaniah's ancestor in the time of, and in the circle of, Hezekiah—but in a priestly family instead of a royal one. In favor of the Hilkiah reading, Ben Zvi points out that both Amariah and Hilkiah are among the ancestors of Ezra (Ezra 7:1), and that Gedaliah, in Ezra 10:18, is a priest who sent away his foreign wife. Thus, all three of the -yah names in Zephaniah's genealogy also appear as priests or their ancestors in the Restoration period, suggesting to Ben Zvi a later origin for Zephaniah's genealogy. He also notes that if indeed there was originally a tradition linking Zephaniah to King Hezekiah, it had disappeared already by the post-biblical period.

Building on the observations of Ben Zvi, it is also possible that "Hezekiah" was the original and that "Hilkiah" is a scribal error or an intentional reworking. Note that Ezra is three generations removed from a Hilkiah (Ezra 7:1) and that Baruch (Book of Baruch 1:1) is four generations removed from a Hilkiah. Perhaps the occurrence of "Hilkiah" in such honorable genealogies attracted the name to Zephaniah's genealogy also, replacing Hezekiah. (Note that Jeremiah is the son of Hilkiahu, a member of a priestly family.)

In the end, it is not possible to decide whether the Hezekiah or the Hilkiah tradition was the original one, or whether two different traditions coexisted.

While most scholars view the genealogy positively, whoever its earliest member may have been, Joseph ibn Caspi (1279–1340) goes against the trend, giving a slightly negative valence to the length of the list. "This prophet related himself to many ancestors—altogether five [including Zephaniah himself]—something that no other prophet did. Perhaps his ancestors were great in wisdom and in prophecy, or perhaps this was required of necessity, but whatever the case, there is no shorter or more honorable genealogy than that of 'Moses, the servant of the Lord' [Deut 34:5; Josh 1:1 and passim]." Ibn Caspi, it would seem, finds Zephaniah's genealogy exaggerated and hence detracting.

Cushi. Although this personal name occurs also in Jer 36:14, several commentators (especially G. Rice) have connected it with the geographical designation Cush = Ethiopia. Thus, for example, Blenkinsopp (*History of Prophecy*, 140) thinks that the genealogy stretching back to King Hezekiah was occasioned by the father's name, Cushi, meaning "Ethiopian" or "Sudanese," and the genealogy, according to Blenkinsopp, was designed by the Deuteronomic school which produced it to counter this hint of foreignness in the prophet's line. This reasoning seems forced, although it is not impossible that all or part of the genealogy was fabricated. It is more likely, however, that Cushi is simply a personal name (cf. "Cush the Benjaminite" in Ps 7:1). I see no reason to link it with Ethiopia or with a dark-skinned person. Nor do I perceive a connection with "Cushites" in 2:12 or "rivers of Cush" in 3:10.

Gedaliah . . . Amariah. The name "Gedaliah" is found in 2 Kings, Jeremiah, Ezra, and Chronicles. Bearers of this name are the leader of the community in Judah after the deportation of Zedekiah, a noble in the time of Zedekiah, a Levite, and a priest who was married to a foreign wife. With the exception of our verse, all occurrences of "Amariah" are in Ezra, Nehemiah, and Chronicles. Bearers of this name are a priest, a descendant of the Levites, a Judean, a head priest at the time of Jehoshaphat, an official at the time of Hezekiah, and an Israelite with a foreign wife.

Names in this pattern, ending with the theophoric element *-yah*, are typical for the late monarchy. Ben Zvi makes the interesting observation, however, that lists of three consecutive names ending with *-yah* occur rarely—in Ezra 7:1 (Amariah appears in 7:3); Neh 11:4 (including Amariah); 12:35; Jer 35:3; 37:13; 51:59 (naming people contemporaneous with Zephaniah). In the Apocryphal Book of Baruch there are also four generations of *-yah* names, ending with "Hilkiah" (lengthened from the "original" in Jer 32:12). Compare Tobit's list of five *-el* names. Ben Zvi suggests that there was a tendency in the late biblical and post-biblical periods to lengthen genealogical lists with names constructed on the same pattern. Perhaps the list in Zeph 1:1 underwent such a lengthening (perhaps as part of the same process which resulted in the change from Hezekiah to Hilkiah mentioned above).

DNF called to my attention that in pre-exilic inscriptions, the spelling tends to be *-yahu*, while the same names are spelled *-yah* in postexilic inscriptions—cf. Z. Zevit, *Matres Lexionis in Ancient Hebrew Epigraphs* (Cambridge, MA: American School of Oriental Research, 1980). If applied to the biblical text, this might support a postexilic dating of the superscription (at least in its present form). But caution must be exercised, for Andersen and Forbes (*Spelling in the Hebrew Bible*, 315) have shown that the orthography of the Minor Prophets as a whole appears late (later than Isaiah, Jeremiah, and Ezekiel), and that there is no significant difference in orthography between the eighth-century minor prophets and those from the sixth century. Hence it is impossible to use orthography as a criterion for dating the individual prophets. The apparent lateness of the present form of the superscription does not, of course, necessarily mean that the entire book is a postexilic composition, nor does it speak to the question of the accuracy of the names contained therein.

In the days of Josiah. The superscription places Zephaniah's activity in the reign of Josiah, 640/39–609 B.C.E. Most scholars accept this dating; a small minority have argued for a postexilic date (Ben Zvi, Smith and Lacheman). Regardless of when the book was actually written or edited, it is set in the time of Josiah and presumably meant to be understood as reflecting that time. The question then becomes whether these chapters can be located more precisely within Josiah's long reign. Most scholars argue, based on Zephaniah's descriptions of religious conditions in Judah, for a date preceding Josiah's reforms in 621; some date Chapter 3 to 612–609 (e.g., Achtemeier). See the INTRODUC-TION for more discussion.

If one accepts the equation of the aforementioned Hezekiah with the Judean king, then the question arises as to the correlation between the number of generations in Zephaniah's genealogy and the genealogy of the kings of Judah. There are four generations between Zephaniah and Hezekiah, and three between Josiah and Hezekiah (Hezekiah reigned 715–687; Manasseh, 687–642; Amon, 642–640; Josiah, 640–609). Abraham Ibn Ezra (11th–12th cent.) solves this discrepancy by pointing out that "there were more than a hundred years between the time that Hezekiah was old enough to sire children and Josiah"—in other words, the long span in the royal genealogy, owing to the lengthy reigns of Hezekiah and especially Manasseh, would allow for an extra generation in other branches of the family tree. Ibn Ezra's explanation receives support from a modern calculation (from DNF) according to which the average age of these Judean kings at the birth of the successor was 34.3 years—somewhat higher than one might expect. If there were four generations in the same time span, the average age of the father at the birth of his first son would be 25.75 years—a quite reasonable figure.

COMMENT

As the NOTES have indicated, the superscription is unusual and has been the subject of much discussion. Doubts have been raised about the authenticity of all or parts of it. Despite its length (or perhaps because of it), we are still unsure of who Zephaniah was or when his book was written. At best, we can say that there was a tradition of a prophet named Zephaniah who lived during the time of Josiah. The superscription cannot predate the book (or at least some form of the book), but it can postdate it. Therefore, even if we conclude that the superscription is late, that does not make the rest of the book equally late.

II. THE ANNOUNCEMENT OF DOOM (1:2–9)

♦

²I will utterly sweep away everything from upon the surface of the
    earth, says the Lord.
³I will sweep away humans and animals;
I will sweep away the birds of the sky and the fish of the sea, and
    the stumbling blocks along with the wicked;
And I will cut off humankind from upon the surface of the
    earth, says the Lord.
⁴I will stretch my hand against Judah and against all the residents
    of Jerusalem,
And I will cut off from this place every vestige of the Baal,
All trace of the idolatrous priests among the priests.
⁵And those who bow down on the rooftops to the host of the
    heavens,
And those who bow down, swearing loyalty to the Lord but
    swearing by their Melekh.
⁶And those who turn aside from after the Lord,
And those who do not seek the Lord and do not inquire of him.
⁷Hush before the Lord God for the Day of the Lord draws near.
The Lord has prepared a sacrifice, he has consecrated his guests.
⁸And on the day of the Lord's sacrifice:
I will punish the officials and the king's sons and all who wear
    foreign clothing.
⁹And I will punish on that day all who leap over the threshold,
Who fill their master's house with lawlessness and fraud.

NOTES

2. *I will utterly sweep.* The translation "sweep" in many English Bibles echoes the sound of the Hebrew consonants. For similar language see Hos 4:3 and Jer 8:13. While the intent of this phrase is clear, its lexical and grammatical forms present problems. Is it possible that the peculiar construction is intended as an allusion, with an ironic reversal of meaning, to the similar-sounding phrase in Mic 2:12?

Normally, one finds an infinite absolute and a finite verb from the same root, but while *ʾasop* is the *qal* infinite absolute from the root *ʾsp*, *ʾasep* appears to be a *hipᶜil* of *swp*—a strange form in itself. A number of suggestions which seek to read both words from the same root are: (1) The finite verb is also from the root *ʾsp* but one *ʾalep* was not written (Rashi; Wellhausen, 150). (2) The second verb can be revocalized as *ʾosep*, making it a *qal* active participle of *ʾsp* (*BHS*). (3) The first word is a *hipᶜil* infinitive of *swp*, on the analogy of the Aramaic *ʾapᶜel* infinitive *ʾaqam[a]* from the root *qwm* (but cf. the note in GKC § 113w). For a fuller discussion see Ben Zvi, 51–53.

Attempts like these to force both words into the same root are not especially satisfying. It seems more plausible that on occasion one may find an infinite absolute plus finite verb from two different but related roots, especially defective roots. Compare Jer 8:13 and Isa 28:28. The effect produces greater assonance, an important feature in prophetic speech, without sacrificing meaning (Gerleman, 2). Or, alternatively, one may note that some defective roots occur in alternate forms: e.g., *ṭwb* and *yṭb*, *ysr* and *ʾsr*. Either of these explanations allows us to view the MT as acceptable, without resorting to complicated emendations. Stylistically related to the alternation of roots in 1:2 may be the alternation in verbal form *(binyan)* in 2:1.

The roots *swp* and *ʾsp* are not semantically distant. *Swp* is commonly used to mean "end, finish" and *ʾsp* also connotes "destruction, ending, withdrawal" in Jud 18:25; Hos 4:3; Isa 60:20; Joel 2:10; 4:15. There is also a third root, *sph*, with a similar sense, easily confused with *swp*; cf. Num 16:26 and Milgrom, *Numbers*, 314 note 57. And Sabottka and Kapelrud entertain a fourth possible root: *ysp*, yielding the meaning "I will again sweep away"—that is, God swept away everything during the Flood and he will do the same again now.

3. *The stumbling blocks along with the wicked.* Hebrew *hammak-šelot* is difficult, as is the entire phrase. The feminine noun is rare (only in Isa 3:6) and the reference here is not apparent. And the force of the particle *ᵓet* is not clear; does it mark the object of *hammakšelot*, a word in apposition to it (see Waltke and O'Connor, 183), or is it a preposition? Furthermore, the insertion of the phrase interrupts the pattern of elements in the verse referring to the natural world.

The general trend has been to take the phrase as meaning "cause the wicked to stumble" although DNF (private communication) points out the strangeness of this, namely, that it is usually the wicked who cause others to stumble. This may be the thinking behind the emendation to *wehikšalti,* "I will cause [the wicked] to stumble," a weak attempt to make the phrase parallel to the following "I will cut off humankind." ("Cause to stumble" seems feeble compared with the other verbs of destruction in this verse.) Alternatively, one might suggest that "the wicked" is in apposition to "the stumbling blocks." But then the feminine form becomes even more problematic. The best solution is to take *ᵓet* as a preposition, "with, along with, associated with."

The feminine form of *hammakšelot* refers, according to some, to the feminine objects connected with idolatry (cf. 2 Kgs 21) or perhaps female deities, like the Queen of Heaven (Jer 7:18; 44:17–18). Roberts considers the phrase a late gloss "that sees the animals mentioned in the preceding line as creatures that led the wicked astray into idolatry."

My own sense is that it might be a kind of gloss but not necessarily a late one; it is a hint that directs us to understand this verse in light of Deuteronomy 4. Deut 4:16–18 warns against making any replica *(tbnyt)* of a man or woman, animal, bird, fish, or crawling thing for purposes of worshiping it. The language of Deuteronomy, as here, is reminiscent of Genesis 1, and it may be that Zephaniah is alluding to the Deuteronomic passage. Deut 4:19 goes on to ban astral worship and contains the terms "host of the heavens" and "bow down" (cf. Zeph 1:5), and Deut 4:25–26 predicts destruction for idolatry. Actually, there may be a double entendre. On one hand Zephaniah is describing a reversal of creation; on the other hand, as becomes clear in the following verses, he is describing the destruction of idolatry. He can achieve this double message because the elements of creation (animals, birds, fish) may also be the elements of idolatry. The "stumbling blocks" can be understood as referring to the replicas (which is feminine in Hebrew). The "stumbling blocks" are, then, not an additional item slated for destruction, but an explanation of the previous items.

Ball also notes the semantic and structural similarity of this passage to Hos 4:1–5, where the natural world suffers the consequences of human misbehavior. The Hosea passage also contains the roots ʾsp and kšl.

4. *Every vestige.* Heb.: "remnant."

Of the Baal. Objects or practices connected with Baal worship.

All trace. Heb.: *šem*, "name." *Šem* has a broader range of meanings than English "name," including "memory, reference, sign, manifestation, essence." Cf. 2 Sam 14:7, in association with šʾryt and Isa 14:22, where, as in our verse, it occurs with šʾr, "remnant"; cf. also Isa 56:5; Exod 3:15; Song 1:3. O'Connor, *HVS*, 242, interprets it as "name/theophanic presence revered by the *komerim*."

The idolatrous priests among the priests. *Kmrym* refers to idolatrous priests; cf. 2 Kgs 23:5; Hos 10:5. For the Akkadian and Aramaic cognates see Tadmor and Cogan, 285. They conclude that the idolatrous priests in 2 Kgs 23:5 "were officiants of West Semitic cults (Baal, Asherah, etc.) typical of the religious amalgam in the Assyrian empire of the West"—that is, priests of foreign deities. These priests had apparently been appointed by the king (Ahlström, 68). Against this explanation, Ben Zvi understands *kmrym* to mean illegitimate priests of YHWH, not priests of an alien deity; that is, priests of YHWH who engage in wrong worship. (For a discussion of the use of *kmrym* in Aramaic see Ben Zvi, 69–71.)

I prefer Ben Zvi's interpretation because it makes v. 4 mirror the structure of vv. 5–6. We have here a series of offenses in an ABAB pattern, in which A is the more severe or more idolatrous and B is the seemingly less severe since it involves syncretism but not complete rejection of YHWH:

1A. vestige of Baal (Baal worship, idolatry),

1B. idolatrous priests (syncretistic practices by priests of YHWH);

2A. astral worship (idolatry),

2B. YHWH worshipers using syncretistic oaths;

3A.   those who turn aside from YHWH (possibly to follow other gods—an active offense),

3B.   those who fail to consult YHWH (a passive offense).

Some translations and commentaries consider *hkhnym*, "the priests," a gloss, since LXX reads only *ton hiereon* (NRSV, NEB, Smith, Roberts). However, as Ball and Roberts point out, the LXX had difficulties with *kmrym*, merely transliterating it in 2 Kgs 23:5 and mistranslating it in Hos 10:5. Others understand the phrase as "the idolatrous priests along with the priests" (NJPS, Ball)—that is, two types of priests are to be cut off (presumably pagan priests and YHWH priests who engage in syncretistic practices). I prefer "the idolatrous priests *among* the priests," rejecting the suggestion that *hkhnym* is a gloss and interpreting the preposition *ᶜm* in the same sense that it is used in Deut 18:1; 1 Sam 2:8; Ps 113:8; Ps 26:4; 88:5. Thus there are not two types of priests slated for destruction, but rather those among the legitimate priests who have become idolatrous.

5. *Swearing loyalty . . . swearing by.*   The nipᶜal of the root *šbᶜ* is used with two different prepositions: *l* and *b*. With *l* the meaning is "to swear loyalty, pledge allegiance to," as in Gen 24:9; Josh 6:22; 1 Kgs 1:13, 51; 2 Kgs 25:24; Isa 19:18. When followed by *b* the meaning is "to swear by, invoke," as in Deut 6:13; 10:20; 1 Sam 20:42, and others (Ehrlich; Ball).

The participles "bowing" and "swearing" each occur twice in this verse, and there is a possibility that one, probably the second occurrence of "bowing," resulted from dittography. (Bowing is mentioned specifically in reference to astral worship in 2 Kgs 17:16.) But I have let both stand.

Their Melekh.   Hebrew *malkām* is a crux with three possible interpretations: (1) Milcom, the Ammonite deity, (2) "their king" as a reference to a human king, or perhaps to Baal or another foreign god, or to the Lord, (3) the Molekh.

(1) Most modern scholars, following the Lucianic recension of the LXX, the Peshitta, and the Vulgate, interpret this as a variant for *Milcom*, the god of the Ammonites. In support of this is the occurrence of the same form, *malkām*, in 2 Sam 12:30 = 1 Chr 20:2 and Jer 49:1, 3, and perhaps Amos 1:15, where it is probably to be understood as "Milcom."

Additional proof of a confusion in the writing of this god's name is found in 1 Kgs 11:7 where *lemolek* is written for "Milcom" (compare 11:5). But why has Zephaniah singled out Milcom in this instance? Milcom is named only in a clearly Ammonite context, or in lists including the gods of Sidon and Moab. The present context does not support "Milcom" as the best interpretation.

(2) The word literally means "their king." As a reference to a human king it is strange, because invoking the name of a king in an oath is otherwise unknown in the Bible (unless Isa 8:21 refers to this practice, which the context makes doubtful although the grammar would support it), although it is found in Akkadian texts (see *CAD* M1 I, 189ff.: *mamītu*). I therefore reject Sweeney's "those sworn to Yhwh and those sworn to their king" (*CBQ* 53, 392), which he justifies indirectly by the prohibition on cursing God and the ruler (Exod 22:27; he neglects to cite 1 Kgs 21:10).

The literal meaning "king" is adopted in the commentary of the Malbim (Meir Loeb ben Yeḥiel Michael, 1809–1879), who finds in this verse three types of people: (1) Baal worshipers, (2) worshipers of YHWH (*hnšbʿym lyhwh*), and (3) those who are loyal neither to Baal nor to the Lord but who follow whatever their king does.

"Their king" may also be a general designation for a pagan deity. The Targum renders it by *bšwm ptkryhwn*, "[swearing by] the name of their idol." (Cf. Targum on Isa 8:21 where the same word is used to render *mlk*.) Sabottka suggests that it is an epithet for Baal. (His suggestion that *mlk* is also an epithet for Baal in 1:8 and 3:15 has little to recommend it.) Ben Zvi understands *mlk* as a reference to YHWH, that is, YHWH wrongly worshiped.

(3) The reference is to the Molekh, a deity or divine epithet (possibly of Phoenician or Syro-Palestinian origin) associated with the ritual of passing children through fire at the Tophet in the valley of Ben Hinnom (Lev 18:21; 20:2–5; 2 Kgs 23:10; Jer 32:35; and elsewhere without specific mention of Molekh). The term *molek* is related to *malik* or *milku*, found in Syrian and Mesopotamian theophoric names. Heider suggests that it is a participial form of *mlk*, meaning "ruler." In biblical names this element may appear as *melek*, as in 2 Kgs 17:31, and once as the sole element (Isa 30:33). From 2 Kgs 17:31, "The Sepharvites burned their

children in the fire to Adrammelech and Anammelech," we may deduce that Molekh or *melek* is not the personal name of a specific god, but rather an epithet that could be applied to any god connected with this fire ritual. It would then mean "the Melekh/Molekh god."

Note that "Molekh" is not a proper noun; it always takes a definite article, and hence I refer to it as "the Molekh." (Note that the definite article is omitted in 1 Kgs 11:7 where the reference is to Milcom.) Therefore it can take a possessive suffix, and I would translate our form "their Melekh," that is, their Molekh god. (The definite article is also affixed to Baal in v. 4 and *passim*. This may also suggest that "the Baal god" is any god with *ba'al* attributes or a *ba'al* element in his name or epithet.)

I favor the Molekh interpretation in our verse, as do Ehrlich, Weinfeld (*UF* 4), Ball, Irsigler, Heider, and Day because of the other literary contexts in which the term is found and their similarity to the present one. The passages closest to ours, in time and tone, are 2 Kgs 17:16–17; 21:3–6; 23:4–10; Jer 19:3; 32:29–35. In all of these the sins of Baal worship, astral worship, and passing children through fire come in close proximity. These are the idolatries of the mid-eighth through seventh centuries, which Josiah sought to eradicate, with only partial success. Worship of Milcom, mentioned in only one of these passages, 2 Kgs 23:13, is an earlier phenomenon, instituted by Solomon (cf. 1 Kgs 11:5–7). Although there may have been remnants of it in Josiah's day (or at least the physical remains of altars), 2 Kings 23 lists it not among the active idolatries of the time, but among the evidence of the wrongdoing of past kings, compared with whom Josiah stands out as a paragon. Finally, the linking of the profanation of YHWH's name with the Molekh-god ritual is found in Lev 18:21 and 20:3. This suggests, as does Zeph 1:5, that uttering God's name was part of the fire ritual or sacrifice to the Molekh god. (For a full discussion of Molekh, and the connection of *mlk* with "the queen [*mlkt*] of heaven," see Weinfeld, *UF* 4; Heider; Day.)

6. The relative clause beginning with *ʾšr* is an equivalent to the nominal clauses employing participles that precede it ("those who bow . . . those who turn aside . . ."). Cf. Andersen, 116. A relative participle may be continued by a *waw*-relative with a suffix form verb. Both the

participle and the perfect verb should be translated in the same tense (Waltke and O'Connor, 630–31). This is not universally recognized in the translations. For example, Exod 9:20–21: *hyr*ʾ . . . *w*ʾšr *l*ʾ *śm lbw*, "he who feared the word of the Lord . . . he who paid no regard to the word of the Lord"; Josh 24:17: *hw*ʾ *hm*ʿlh . . . *w*ʾšr ʿśh, "it was he who brought us up . . . and who performed." Also Exod 21:12–13; Mic 3:2–3; and cf. Amos 8:14; Mic 3:5.

7. The prophet speaks in his own voice here, resuming the words of God after "And on the day of the Lord's sacrifice" in v. 8.

The Day of the Lord. This term occurs numerous times in prophetic writing (Isa 13:6, 9; Ezek 13:5; Joel 1:15; 2:1, 11; 3:4; 4:14; Amos 5:18, 20; Obad 15; Mal 3:23. See also Isa 2:12; Ezek 30:3; Zech 14:1; Isa 34:8; Jer 46:10; Isa 22:5; and, the only non-prophetic passages, Lam 1:12; 2:22). Zephaniah uses a number of variations: "the day of the wrath of the Lord," "the day of the Lord's sacrifice." There have been different speculations about the origin of this expression and the concept which it embodies (summarized in *IDBSup*, 209–10, *TDOT* VI, 29–31, *ABD* II:81–85, and Paul, 182–86). In most prophetic texts it appears to be a time, near at hand, when God will alter the current situation. Everson's definition (*JBL* 93) is the broadest and therefore the safest: a prophetic interpretation of momentous events in the past, present, or future. Attempts to narrow the definition do not account for all of the passages in which the term is found. A number of scholars view the term as a commonly known one which prophets like Amos and Zephaniah reverse, turning it into a day of destruction for Israel instead of a day of deliverance from her enemies, as it was previously understood. But Weiss (*HUCA* 37) holds that it is not a pre-prophetic concept, but originated with Amos. Whatever its origin, the Day of the Lord as expressed by some of the prophets includes judgment both upon Israel and upon nations. According to Zephaniah 1, Judah will be the primary victim, but the Philistines are also destroyed on this day according to 2:3–4. Likewise, Isaiah 13, Obad 15, and Ezekiel 7 include other nations among the casualties of that day. It seems best, then, to posit that the concept of the Day of the Lord included judgment upon both Israel and other nations, and that either Israel or the other nations could be emphasized, depending on the rhetorical needs of the speaker. See also the NOTE on 2:4.

A *sacrifice.*   Heb. *zbḥ,* the type of sacrifice in which part was offered up to God and part was eaten by the priests and the bringer of the sacrifice. The image is metaphoric: the sacrifice will be the people of Judah. Compare the same image used in reference to other nations, also in connection with a day of the Lord or a day of vengeance in Isa 34:6; Jer 46:10; Ezek 39:17.

Consecrated his guests.   The participants in the sacrificial meal are in a state of purity; the sacrifice is imminent. References to guests at a sacrifice are found in 1 Sam 9:13, 22; 1 Kgs 1:41, 49. There is no apparent identification for this part of the metaphor, although some have sought a role for Israel's enemies here. It simply completes the picture of God's preparations. It also makes use of the double entendre in *qdš,* "consecrate," which also means "to prepare for battle" (Jer 6:4; Joel 4:9). The image of God's sacrifice occurs also in Jer 46:10 (slaughter of enemies), Isa 34:6 (slaughter of enemies), and Ezek 39:17–19 (Gog). The metaphor may play upon a natural bond between sacrifice and punishment or war since both involve slaughter, the spilling of blood, etc. Zephaniah, however, has used it somewhat differently from others; instead of representing the slaughter of Israel's enemies, it signals the slaughter of Judah itself. This becomes clear in v. 8; in v. 7 the reader or listener cannot quite resolve the metaphor. Is Judah the sacrifice or the guest who will witness the sacrifice?

8. *The king's sons.*   If Zephaniah prophesied early in the reign of Josiah, who came to the throne at the age of eight (2 Kgs 22:1), this could not refer to the children of Josiah. Perhaps it refers to the brothers of the late king, Amon, who exercised influence over the young Josiah (so NJPS), or, better, the royal family in general. Or, if one takes *ben melek* as an official title (cf. Brin; Hestrin, 22), it could indicate the government officials, the class against whom criticism is often leveled by prophets. LXX reads *ton oikon tou basileos,* "the king's house(hold)." Hebrew *bny* and *byt* are sometimes interchanged in the LXX—cf. Jer 16:15; Ezek 2:3; 1 Chr 2:10; Gen 45:11; Exod 16:31; Josh 17:17; 18:5; Hos 1:7.

Foreign clothing.   Signifying either the expensive and snobbish tastes of imported clothing or the vestments of Baal worship, as in 2 Kgs 10:22.

9. *Leap over the threshold.*   This is usually interpreted in light of

1 Sam 5:5, which mentions that the priests of Dagon and all who enter the temple of Dagon do not tread upon the threshold *(mptn)* of Dagon at Ashdod. In other words, this is another syncretistic practice, in this case borrowed from the Philistines. The Targum's "all who walk in the laws of the Philistines" reflects this interpretation. An alternative explanation sees the leaping over the threshold as a general superstitious practice, since in many cultures demons were thought to congregate near entrances and doorways (so Smith, *ICC*, 208 and Donner). Less likely is Gerleman's "die auf das Podium steigen" (to mount the platform on which the statue of the god was located), since *mptn* elsewhere in the Bible clearly means "threshold" (e.g., Ezek 9:3; 10:4). Medieval Jewish commentaries suggest that the reference is to the rich and powerful barging into the homes of the poor to collect taxes and debts.

Their master's house. This may refer to the Lord's Temple (so the Ancient Versions), if the first part of the verse refers to a pagan practice; or to the king's palace, if the verse is speaking of economic oppression.

COMMENT

Zephaniah opens his prophecy with a vociferous announcement of doom. It begins with a broad panorama—all living beings—and moves to a narrowing focus—Judah and Jerusalem, and those who engage in idolatry or syncretistic religious practices. Zephaniah speaks specifically of three types of idolatrous worship which have three loci: Baal worship, conducted in the Temple; astral worship, practiced on rooftops; and the ritual dedicated to the Molekh, performed in the valley of Ben Hinnom. Baal worship, which could be a general designation for all worship of foreign deities, goes back to the early monarchy and was the result of contact with Phoenicians and other northwest Semitic groups. Astral worship, which may also have earlier origins, was practiced in Mesopotamia and seems to have gained popularity in the period of Assyrian dominance. The origin of the Molekh is unknown (perhaps Phoenician, although Weinfeld [*UF* 4] seems to connect it here with the Aramean-Assyrian cult, the worship of Hadad/Adad and Anat/Ishtar). All of these were presumably syncretistic, i.e., the participants performed these idolatrous acts in addition to normative Judean worship of YHWH. In

v. 6 Zephaniah mentions an additional group, those who have abandoned the worship of YHWH altogether.

The picture of Judean religious practice that Zephaniah provides is similar to that which is ascribed to Manasseh in 2 Kings 21 and which Josiah sought to eradicate in 2 Kings 23. It is a combination of earlier Canaanite or Phoenician practices and later Assyrian ones, which were combined syncretistically with Judean practices. Although the prophets, purists that they were, railed against such syncretisms, it is quite understandable that Judah would be open to foreign influence in all spheres of life and that the upper classes, like upper classes everywhere, would imitate chic foreign lifestyles, especially those of a great power like Assyria. (There is no evidence that Assyria imposed its religion on areas over which it had political control, but it seems likely that inhabitants of vassal states would have found the "superior" power's religious practices, like other aspects of its culture, attractive.) The fact that Josiah was able to end these syncretistic practices testifies not only to his own strength, but also to the waning influence of Assyria. Zephaniah's prophecy would have given support to Josiah's reforms.

Verses 2 and 3 not only provide a rhetorical trumpet blast of chastisement, but also, by playing on the creation motif, introduce a significant theological theme. As several scholars have noted, there are numerous points of contact between Zeph 1:2–3 and Genesis 1. The list of the doomed—humans, animals, birds of the sky, fish of the sea— reverses the order in which these were created according to Genesis 1. And the same items appear in Gen 1:26 where humans are given control over the fish of the sea, birds of the sky, animals, all the land, and all that crawls on the land. Zephaniah also plays on ʾadam and ʾadamah, "humans and earth," as does Gen 2:7. The twice-repeated "surface of the earth" harks back to Gen 6:7 and 7:23, God's decision to erase humans from the surface of the earth. The phrase also occurs in Gen 2:6.

These observations are nicely interpreted by M. de Roche as a reversal of creation. Indeed, this is so; but the implications of this (and also the references to the Flood, which de Roche minimizes) go beyond a simple literary allusion.

Zephaniah is not alone in speaking of a reversal of creation. Job 3 uses this motif for a different purpose, to erase the day of his birth—i.e., to undo a particular point in time. Hos 4:1–3 and Jer 4:23–28 use it in a manner similar to Zephaniah. Here it is all-encompassing, for it is not one personal aspect of creation that the prophet wishes could be annulled, but all of creation which he is certain will be imminently overturned. Jeremiah sees the end of the physical world; Hosea and Zephaniah warn of the destruction of animate beings.

J. D. Levenson has investigated the meaning of creation in biblical theology, and has shown that its basic thrust is to demonstrate the mastery of God over the universe and the establishment of order out of chaos. This benevolent order in the world, however, is fragile—always in danger of dissolving. In fact, its fragility becomes obvious in the Flood story, when, for all practical purposes, the world is destroyed and re-created. It is not, then, creation itself that is permanent; permanence is achieved by God's covenant with Noah that the world will never again be destroyed (cf. Levenson, 48). Isa 54:9–10 can therefore use this covenant as an absolute standard of permanent security, even in the face of what appears to be total annihilation.

> "For this is to me like the waters [or: days] of Noah. As I swore that the waters of Noah would never again flood the earth, so I swear that I will not be angry with you or rebuke you. For the mountains may move and the hills be shaken, but my loyalty shall never move from you and my covenant of alliance will not be shaken . . ."

God's relationship with Israel, says Isaiah, is as firm as his covenant with Noah. It is significant that Isaiah did not cite God's covenant with Abraham or with David, but rather that most primary of covenants, the one with Noah.

Unlike Isaiah, Zephaniah abrogates God's covenant with Noah. What is the implication of such a powerful statement? That the benevolent order that God has instituted at creation, and that Israel has now come to take for granted, will come to an end. Why will it come to an end? Is not God's promise to Noah unconditional?

Although he does not mention Zephaniah, Levenson provides a way of understanding this passage. In a chapter entitled "Chaos Neutralized in Cult," Levenson discusses the cultic associations with creation, especially Temple building and the Sabbath. He suggests that

> the creative ordering of the world has become something that humanity can not only witness and celebrate, but something in which it can also take part. Among the many messages of Gen 1:1–2:3 is this: it is through the cult that we are able to cope with evil, for it is the cult that builds and maintains order, transforms chaos into creation, ennobles humanity, and realizes the kingship of the God who has ordained the cult and commanded that it be guarded and practiced. It is through obedience to the directives of the divine master that his good world comes into existence. [127]

If, as Levenson suggests, the cult enables its practitioners to participate in creation, to renew it, to show the ongoing triumph of benevolent order over chaos, then what happens when the cult is misused or corrupted? The result must be the breakdown of creation, the removal of benevolent order, and the subsequent failure of Israel to thrive. If God's creation is to be maintained, the cult must be rid of those who undermine it—and they are listed in the subsequent verses: those who worship Baal, bow to the Queen of Heaven, swear by their Melekh, turn away from the Lord. Zephaniah is not merely alluding to the reversal of creation as the most catastrophic image of destruction; he is telling his audience that the religious failure of Judah means the end of the world order.

The religious failure of Judah is not in breaking the link between cult and creation, but in subverting the cult in a slide toward paganism. Not only are pagan cults often associated with procreation (fertility), but in the case of Zephaniah, as I have suggested in the NOTE to 1:3, we may have a more specific allusion to the use of elements of creation (humans, animals, etc.) in the form of replicas for idolatrous worship. Zephaniah, then, is saying two things: that God will destroy his creation, which has, in essence, been destroyed already by the perversion of the cult; and that God will destroy the replicas of creation that represent a false cult.

The specific failure that the prophet criticizes is syncretistic practices, including the worship of pagan deities like Baal, pagan rituals like the

Molekh rite, and astral worship. The same situation is reflected during the time of Manasseh (2 Kgs 21:1–7), countermanded by Josiah (2 Kgs 23:4–5), and later criticized by Jeremiah (Jer 8:2; 19:13). There is no suggestion that the Judeans ever abandoned worship of the Lord totally; only that they combined it with all manner of foreign practices, something that the prophets found repugnant but that the people probably considered relatively unproblematic. This, of course, is what made the prophets' mission so difficult.

The cultic failures of the Judeans are, as it were, counterbalanced by God's performance of his own sacrifice. His Day is near and his sacrifice is about to take place. The prophet, like a herald, announces the Day of the Lord, which is here the Day of the Lord's Sacrifice and the Day of the Wrath of the Lord. Because sacrifice is associated with sanctification and cult, it nicely contrasts what the Judeans were doing with what God wants to have done; and because it is associated with slaughter and blood, it is an apt image for God's punishment of all who deserve it. In this double image, the Judeans move from those consecrated to those punished. The progression of the punished moves from members of the royal court to the wealthy business people to the owners of estates. Ultimately the disaster will strike all the inhabitants of Jerusalem.

III. A Description of Doom (1:10–18)

◆

¹⁰And on that day there shall be, says the Lord,
A loud outcry from the Fish Gate,
And a wail from the Mishneh,
And a great crash from the Hills.
¹¹Wail, dwellers of the Makhtesh,
For gone are all the merchants,
Cut off are all who weigh out silver.
¹²And at that time I will search Jerusalem with lamps,
And I will punish the people who are congealing on their dregs,
Who think to themselves, "The Lord will not make things better
    or worse."
¹³Their wealth shall become pillage,
And their homes desolation.
They shall build houses but not inhabit them;
They shall plant vineyards but not drink their wine.
¹⁴Near is the great day of the Lord, nearing very swiftly.
The sound of the day of the Lord: bitterly shrieks then a warrior.
¹⁵A day of wrath is that day:
A day of distraint and distress,
A day of devastation and desolation,
A day of darkness and gloom,
A day of clouds and dense fog.
¹⁶A day of trumpet blast and siren,
Against the fortified cities and against the lofty corner towers.

¹⁷And I will bring distress upon people.
They shall walk like the blind because they have sinned against
the Lord.
Their blood shall be splattered like dust and their fleshy parts like
dung.
¹⁸Neither their silver nor their gold will be able to save them on
the day of the wrath of the Lord.
The entire earth will be consumed by the fire of his passion;
For a total, indeed terrible, end will he make of all the
inhabitants of the earth.

NOTES

10. *Fish Gate*. This gate has been located in the north wall of Jerusalem. According to Neh 3:3 and 12:39 it was located between the Old Gate and the Sheep Gate. 2 Chr 33:14 dates its existence at least as far back as Manasseh. It was most likely so named because it served as the entry to the Jerusalem fish market (cf. Neh 13:16). LXX's "gate of those who slay" is a misreading of *hrgym* for *hdgym*.

Mishneh. The "Second Quarter." A residential area on the Western Hill or Upper City of Jerusalem inhabited by the upper classes. It overlooked the Temple Mount and was near the main commercial center. Archaeological evidence suggests that it was already settled by the time of Hezekiah and was incorporated into the city by him when he reinforced the city walls (cf. Mazar, 2.591, and Avigad, *The Upper City of Jerusalem*, 54–60). According to 2 Kgs 22:14, the prophetess Huldah resided there. The Targum renders it "Ophel," the ridge extending south between the Kidron and Tyropoeon valleys. LXX and Vulgate apparently thought the reference was to a second gate.

The Hills. The context suggests that this should refer to a specific geographical location, but its identity is unknown.

For similar phraseology, applied to different geographical locations, see Jer 51:54 and also Jer 48:3–5.

11. *Wail*. The root *yll*, here in the *hipˤil*, has been connected to funerary lamentation. However, as noted in *TDOT* VI, 82–87, it occurs only once outside of the prophetic corpus (Deut 32:10), and in the

prophets it is always used in connection with a communal catastrophe. It thus does not connote ordinary mourning, but rather the public reaction to extraordinary, large-scale destruction.

Makhtesh. Probably the lower area later known as the Tyropoeon Valley that separates the Upper City from the Temple Mount. The word means "mortar" or "depression." According to this verse, the merchants conducted their business here. The Targum reads "Kidron wadi."

Gone. Heb. *nidmah* from the root *dmh* meaning "stop, end." LXX interprets it from the homophonous root meaning "to be like, similar"; Vulgate takes it from *dmm*, "to be silent."

Merchants. Heb. *kena'an.* For this meaning of "Canaanite" see Hos 12:8; Isa 23:8; Ezek 16:29; 17:4; Prov 31:24; Zech 14:21.

Weigh out silver. The Versions are somewhat inexact about the phrase, rendering "excited by silver" (LXX), "involved with silver" (Vulgate), "rich in property" (Targum). As Smith (*ICC*, 200) points out, weighing out silver does not refer specifically to money changers, or, I would add, silversmiths, but to all merchants engaged in financial transactions. In this sense, the rendering "bearing/laden with silver" (cf. KJV, House) captures the essence of the meaning if not the grammatical form (which is active, not passive).

12. *Search Jerusalem with lamps.* The image is one of God carefully searching into every dark corner. None can hide from God; all sinners will be discovered. For other references to God's searching out individuals see Amos 9:3; Jer 5:1; Ezek 22:30; and especially Ps 139:12: "Even darkness is not dark to you; and night is as light as the day . . ." The Targum, troubled by the anthropomorphism of this verse, renders it less directly as "I will appoint searchers and they will search the inhabitants of Jerusalem like those who search with lamps."

Congealing on their dregs. This image is drawn from the process of wine making. New wine is allowed to sit upon the sediment of the grapes long enough to fix its color and body. Then it is drawn off, before it becomes too thick and syrupy, and subject to mold. (For a fuller description see Clark, *BT* 32.) The uncommon word *qp'ym*, "solidify, freeze, coagulate, congeal," suggests that the wine has sat too long on its lees and thickened too much—that is, the people have become mired in their drinking and indulgent lifestyle. The image captures the decadence of Jerusalem's upper classes.

The wine-making image is used for a different effect in Jer 48:11: "Moab has been at ease from his youth, settled on his dregs; he has not been emptied from vessel to vessel, nor has he gone into exile. Therefore his flavor has remained and his bouquet is unspoiled." Jeremiah's image is of wine left undisturbed, not drawn off too soon, so that its flavor has set properly. Zephaniah's image is of wine left too long, beyond the proper time, so that it has become too thick. (Clark, *BT* 32, interprets the Jeremiah passage differently.)

This phrase has had widely differing renderings, both in ancient and in modern times. The LXX reads "who look with contempt upon their commandments"; the Old Latin has "who are scornful, not guarding the commandment"; the Targum reads "who in tranquility enjoy their property." Whether through misunderstanding of the text or intentional interpretation, these Versions have caught the gist, if not the literal meaning. A number of modern English translations (NRSV, NJPS) have "the people who rest complacently." This appears to be a conflation of the suggested emendation of *š°nnym* for *°nšym* (cf. BHS), probably influenced by Jer 48:11, and an interpretation of *qp°ym* which is not apparent to me. There is little reason to accept the emendation to *š°nnym*, for there is no manuscript evidence for it and, as mentioned above, the image in Jer 48:11 is quite different from ours. However, like the Ancient Versions, the modern translations convey the general idea of the phrase.

Will not make things better or worse. Lit. "will cause neither good nor evil." The idea is that these people think that God is powerless to act. This is perhaps worse than the more common image of people who think that God will always continue to protect them. Cf. Jer 5:12; Ps 14:1. Another view is that God is indifferent (DNF).

13. *Build houses . . . plant vineyards.* This is the formulaic way of saying "establish a community" (cf. Deut 20:5–10; 28:30; Isa 65:21–23; Jer 24:6; 29:5–7; 31:3–4; 35:7; 42:10; 45:4; Ezek 28:26; 36:36; Amos 5:11; 9:14; Ps 107:36–38; Eccl 2:4. According to Deut 20:5–10, these activities are so important that they warrant a deferment from the army. Our verse is closest to the curses of Deut 28:30; the warning that the existing

community will soon go out of existence. (For more on this formula and its usages see Berlin, "Jeremiah 29:5–7.") Zephaniah nicely combines this formula with the images of wealth and of the dregs in the previous verses.

14. *The sound.* Hebrew: *qwl*, may also be rendered "Hark!" I have rendered "the sound" to bring out the idea that the day brings with it the sound of shrieking.

The language is difficult and may have suffered some corruption. I follow the masoretic phrase division, against most modern commentaries, which read "Hark, the Day of the Lord is bitter; there shrieks a warrior." (For the idea of a bitter day, see Amos 8:10.)

Bitterly. For *mr* as an adverb describing vocal expression, see Isa 33:7. Kutler, *UF* 16, makes a case for *mrr* = "strong." He suggests that our verse means that the Day of the Lord will be so strong/bitter that even a warrior shrieks.

Shrieks. *Ṣrḥ* is attested in Isa 42:13 (also in association with *gibbor*) and in the Akkadian cognate *ṣarāḫu.*

Then. Hebrew *šam* is an adverb with demonstrative force. While it usually has a locational sense, it may on occasion have a temporal sense (so Bolle, cf. also Waltke and O'Connor, 307, 657–58). Thus *šam* may also be rendered "then," as in Prov 8:27; Job 35:12.

A warrior. Even an outstanding soldier will shriek in fright. Ball and Ben Zvi take *gbwr* as a divine title or a reference to God, who would then be the subject of this clause.

A widely cited emendation is *qal yom YHWH meraṣ weḥaš miggibbor,* "The Day of the Lord is faster than a runner; fleeter than a warrior." However, there is no support for this, and, as Roberts observed, its thought would be redundant.

The Versions also had considerable difficulty with this verse: LXX has "and harsh, is appointed a powerful one"; the Vulgate has "oppressed there is the strong"; the Targum has "and he cries there, the hero put [to death]."

Finally, I raise the possibility of another parsing of the syntax. According to the pattern of other similar *qol* references, e.g., Gen 4:10; Song 5:2, which is *qol* + X + *participle*, X is the subject of the participle. Hence our verse would mean "Hark, the Day of the Lord bitterly shrieks . . ."

15. A *day of wrath* . . . The Day of the Lord is described in anaphoric lines containing pairs of lexically associated words, several containing paronomasia. The idea of a day of divine wrath also occurs in Isa 13:9; Ezek 7:19; Prov 11:4; Job 21:30. The Vulgate's translation of this phrase, *Dies irae dies illa,* forms the opening of the medieval hymn by Thomas of Celano formerly used in the Catholic Requiem Mass.

The terms for distress, devastation, and so forth are common. For extensive references see Ball, 84–88, and Ben Zvi, 122–24.

A *day of darkness.* The darkness in the last part of the verse has been linked with physical phenomena like a solar eclipse or the darkening before a storm. These are portents of or preliminaries to disaster. Heavy clouds are also associated with the theophany (Exod 19:18; 20:18). Both the portent of disaster and the appearance of God inhere in the image that Zephaniah is trying to create. See also Joel 2:2; Isa 8:22; Amos 5:18, 20; Ezek 34:12.

16. A *day of trumpet blast and siren.* The *šopar,* "ram's horn," was used in battle and to give an alarm within a city. Cf., for example, Jer 20:16; Hos 5:8; Amos 3:6. Here it seems to refer to the blast of the enemy in preparation for an attack.

Corner towers. The towers at the corners of the wall. Many royal fortresses in the eighth and seventh centuries were rectangular with a tower at each corner. The image in v. 16 is similar to Josh 6:5, 20.

17. *I will bring distress.* The word *whṣrty* is a *hipʿil* form of the root *ṣrr,* "to cause trouble, bring to dire straits," but it is also possible to see here a play on the word *nṣr,* "besieged" (cf. Isa 1:8). This would extend the war imagery, which indeed continues at the end of v. 17.

Upon people. Hebrew *ʾdm* means "human beings" and is often used to distinguish humans from non-humans. Its usage is somewhat strange here. I see it as refocusing the picture on the human inhabitants after having focused on the cities and their architectural features. Many commentators see here a universal destruction (*ʾdm* = humankind), an interpretation supported by v. 18 "the entire earth" and by the universality of the destruction at the beginning of the chapter. I am in agreement. Ben Zvi argues for a more restricted destruction. He notes that *ʾdm* need not refer to all human beings, but just to a group of them, and that *ʾrṣ*, "land, earth," may mean "Judah" (cf. Joel 1:14). The destruction would then be limited to Judah.

Like the blind. The imagery of darkness (cf. v. 15) returns with a new twist. The people will stumble blindly, unguided by God's commandments. Cf. Deut 28:28–29; Isa 59:10; Lam 4:14.

Splattered like dust. Literally, "poured out." The image is unusual. The verb *špk* is used of blood, and also of *ʿpr*, "dust" (Lev 14:41), but blood is usually poured out like water (Ps 79:3), not like dust. The combination of this particular tenor and vehicle, along with the accompanying "fleshy parts like dung," creates the vivid image of carnage strewn over a broad area. The word *ʿpr*, "dust," means fine particles of soil, rock, or similar material. It has the sense here of "dirt." Dirt and dung are common, widespread, and filthy. The massacre will be so great that corpses will not be left intact; the remains will be in small fragments—specks and clumps—scattered over the landscape. Cf. Ps 18:43: "I ground them fine as windswept dust; I trod them flat as dirt of the streets" (NJPS).

Dust is also associated with death and the grave—cf. Ps 22:30 and *passim*. For other associations see Hillers, "Dust: Some Aspects of Old Testament Imagery."

Fleshy parts like dung. The exact meaning of *lḥmm* is uncertain. It occurs only here and in Job 20:23. It has been connected to Arabic *laḥm*, "flesh, meat," or to the verb *lḥm*, "to press together," hence "intestines, bowels." Whatever the exact nuance of the word, it would seem to refer to body tissue, parallel to the body fluid indicated by "blood."

O'Connor, *HVS*, 247, graphically renders "Their bloody guts are poured out like dung in dust." He accepts Sabottka's reading of *lḥ*, "sap, strength," with *lḥm* a possible by-form of it, and combines the two parts of the parallelism, thereby reuniting the parts of the idea which he feels were broken up in order to form the parallelism. In this case, such a recombining does not seem to me to reflect the underlying idea nor to do justice to the parallelism.

18. *Neither their silver . . .* Cf. Ezek 7:19 for an almost identical phrase which Ezekiel seems to have borrowed from Zephaniah.

The entire earth. Hebrew *ʾrṣ* means either "land" or "earth" and it is not always easy to decide which. In light of the beginning of Chapter 1, the prophecy against the nations in Chapter 2, and my discussion of the Day of the Lord (NOTE to v. 7), I take ʾrṣ to mean "earth" in this verse. While the main focus of God's wrath is Judah, the Judeans are warned that they cannot escape because God's wrath will encompass the whole earth.

COMMENT

The Day of the Lord is described in graphic detail. Destruction spreads through Jerusalem's business district and wealthy residential areas, from northwest (the Fish Gate) to southwest (the Mishneh) to south and southeast. The destruction is characterized by its sound—wailing and crashing. Sound is also a feature of the day itself (v. 14), a day of trumpet blast and siren (v. 16). Along with sound comes sight, or the absence of clear sight—darkness and gloom, clouds and fog, and finally people walking like the blind. In contrast to this black and gray is the bright and multicolored effect of splattered blood (v. 17), gold and silver (v. 18), and the fiery conflagration. Chapter 1 ends as it began, with the destruction of the whole earth.

The underlying image is one of war, commingled with theophany and sacrifice. But it is the aftermath that is emphasized. Homes will be destroyed, possessions plundered. The victims will wander blindly and will be massacred; the whole land will be consumed.

If we accept the definition of the Day of the Lord as referring to a momentous historical event that the prophet seeks to interpret theologically, and if we date Zephaniah's prophecy to the time of Josiah, then the overarching momentous event is the deterioration of the Assyrian empire, especially following the death of Ashurbanipal in 628. (It is not necessary that the "day" be a short-term event, covering a day or a week; it might just as well refer to a longer period without clear boundaries.) The decline and fall of a great empire is a time of turmoil, of the upsetting of the world order, of a realignment among other world powers. (It may be compared to the breakup of the USSR in our own time.) On one hand, it must have raised many Judean hopes for autonomy and expansion. On the other hand, it was a dangerous time for a small kingdom, a time to be nervous about who the heir to the Assyrian empire might be. Moreover, in the eyes of the prophets, Judah did not deserve to gloat, for it was religiously corrupt. The idolatrous practices of the enemy had infiltrated the Judean court and Temple. In this sense, Judah was no better than the other nations and would share their fate. Only the faithful would escape the cataclysm, as we are told in Chapter 2.

IV. The Last Chance to Repent (2:1–4)

◆

2 ¹Gather together, gather like straw, O unwanted nation.
²Before the decree's birth—the day is fleeting like chaff—
Before there comes over you the fierce wrath of the Lord,
Before there comes over you the day of wrath of the Lord.
³Seek the Lord, all you humble of the land, who have performed
     his command.
Seek righteousness, seek humility.
Perhaps you will be hidden on the day of the wrath of the Lord.
⁴For Gaza shall be abandoned,
And Ashkelon become a desolation.
Ashdod, at noon they will drive her out,
And Ekron will be uprooted.

NOTES

2:1 *Gather together.* The root *qšš*, "gather," is a denominative from *qaš*, "straw, stubble," and is used in the sense of gathering straw or wood. It is not generally used for assembling people and does not appear elsewhere in the MT in the *hitpaᶜel (hitpolel)*. This has led some scholars to propose emendations like *hitbošešu*, "be ashamed," or *hitqaddešu*, "consecrate yourselves," or to derive the word from *yqš*, "lay a snare"— but there is no support for these. The word as it is found in the MT makes a nice soundplay with *nksp* in the following phrase and a semantic connection with *kmwṣ* in v. 2. Furthermore, although unusual, it is

95

completely grammatical. One must assume, following the methodology of Meir Weiss *(The Bible from Within)*, that it was chosen intentionally for a specific effect. (See the following note for my explanation.)

Gather. The root *qšš* is repeated but in the *qal*, a form also not found outside of this occurrence. The use of the same root in different verbal conjugations is a feature of parallelistic discourse—cf. Berlin, *Dynamics*, 36–40. I have tried to capture the specificity of these verbs, that is, their association with straw, by translating "gather like straw." Several scholars (Hunter, Roberts) see in this image the worthlessness of the people—they are just so much straw or stubble. (This is echoed in the following "unwanted nation.") But the connotation of "straw" is not so much "worthlessness" (this is the connotation of "chaff"), but flammability. When "straw" is used metaphorically, it usually means quickly burned—cf. Isa 5:24; 47:14; Joel 2:5; and especially Exod 15:7. The preceding verse (1:18) told us that God's wrath would consume the world like fire; now we have Judah, strawlike, easily ignited, with no defense against the imminent conflagration.

O unwanted nation. The Hebrew has the definite article before "nation," employing it to mark a definite addressee who is addressed in the vocative (Waltke and O'Connor, 247). Who is the nation being addressed? Most probably it is Judah, although a few commentaries have suggested that it is the Philistines (connecting this verse with v. 4).

Unwanted. Hebrew *nksp* in our verse has a tradition of being interpreted to mean "be ashamed," as in Aramaic, where the word connotes "to become pale from embarrassment." Others interpret it in its more normative Hebrew meaning, "to desire, to long for, to be eager for." The sense would then be "O nation not desired [by God]" or "O nation not desiring [God]." The *nipʿal* may have both an active and a passive meaning. The word *nksp* recalls 1:18, "Neither their silver [*kspm*]."

2. *Before the decree's birth.* This phrase and the next one are difficult. The Versions either translate literally or paraphrase. The only other place where *ṭrm* does not precede a finite verb is Hag 2:15, where it precedes an infinitive, as in our passage, and Isa 17:14, where it precedes a noun. The Isaiah passage appears to have some loose, if tenuous, connections with this one. Both address nations, Isa 17:13 also

contains the word *kmwṣ*, and Isa 17:14 has *blhh* (cf. Zeph 1:18 *nbhlh*). Compare also Hos 13:3.

Smith prefers to read *thyw ldq*, "before you become fine dust." This eliminates many of the problems but finds no support in manuscripts or the Versions.

A more popular emendation (BHS and many modern translations; cf. Roberts) is *l(ʾ) tdḥqw* in place of *ldt ḥq*, yielding "before you are driven away." This makes better sense, but the root *dḥq* is uncommon, found only in Jud 2:18 and Joel 2:8, meaning "oppress" or "push." It does not quite mean "drive away." NEB reads "before you are sent far away," apparently emending to *trḥqw*; cf. R. L. Smith, *Micah-Malachi*. O'Connor translates "Before the womb comes to term," taking *ḥq* as related to Arabic *ḥuqq*, "hollow, cavity" (see also Sabottka).

The more the suggestions and emendations multiply, the less certain any one of them appears. Despite the fact that the MT does not yield good sense, I let it stand for lack of a convincing alternative.

The day is fleeting like chaff. This presents syntactic and semantic difficulties. I have translated as literally as possible, although the sense is not altogether clear. The verb is in the perfect, although an imperfect or participle would have been preferred. The Versions have problems with *ywm*; LXX and Peshitta omit it and Targum and Vulgate reconstitute its syntax. NRSV translates this and the preceding phrase "before you are driven away like the drifting chaff." Roberts is similar. This makes the most coherent image of a probably corrupt text. It is impossible, however, to ascertain exactly what the MT sought to communicate.

Before . . . the fierce wrath. The Hebrew has the negative particle in this and the following clause. The result is a kind of double negative for emphasis. Alternatively, the syntax may be interpreted as "in order that . . . not." That is, in order that the wrath of God not overtake you (Ball, 118; Gerleman, 28).

This verse ends with two similar clauses. Some consider this redundant, or even an error resulting from dittography. It may, on the other hand, have been intentional. Some manuscripts omit the first clause, but whether this resulted from haplography or not is impossible to say. As the MT stands, its effect is to increase the anaphora, which Zephaniah uses on several occasions, and to bring into sharper focus "the day of the wrath of the Lord" as being the time at which "the fierce wrath of the Lord" will become manifest. The Hebrew has *ywm'p* here, a synonym of *ywm 'brh* in 1:15.

3. *Seek the Lord.* Compare 1:6: "Those who do not seek the Lord."

Humble of the land. This term appears in the prophets and in Psalms (e.g. Amos 8:4; Isa 11:4; Ps 76:10). It may be used for the lower economic classes or for those who are faithful to God's commandments.

Who have performed . . . The more usual syntax of a dependent relative clause in which the subject of the relative clause is the same as in the main clause is *'sr* + verb + object. Here we find *'sr* + object + verb. This order emphasizes "his command" and puts it a bit closer to its antecedent, "the Lord." The prophet holds out a last-minute hope of escape for those who have obeyed God's law.

Seek righteousness . . . These words are reminiscent of Mic 6:8: "doing justice, loving faithfulness, and walking humbly with your God."

4. Philistia, Judah's neighbor to the west, is doomed. The verse is full of consonance, especially at its beginning and end: "Gaza (*'zh*) shall be abandoned (*'zwbh*)" and "Ekron (*'qrwn*) will be uprooted (*t'qr*)." Ball, 120, attempts to catch the consonance by translating "For Gaza shall be ghastful . . . and Ekron shall be extirpated." Cf. also Christensen's "For Gaza shall be ghastly." These translations sacrifice meaning for soundplay (DNF).

Each colon begins with the name of a city, thereby producing a kind of anaphora which hammers out the point that each city will, in turn, meet with destruction. The syntax of the rest of the colon varies, perhaps to avoid monotony, although most translations do not convey this.

There were five Philistine cities: Gaza, Ashdod, Ashkelon, Gath, and Ekron (cf. Josh 13:3); but when they are enumerated in the speeches of the later prophets, no more than four are mentioned and the one omitted is always Gath. Our verse, moving from south to north, lists Gaza, Ashkelon, Ashdod, and Ekron. Amos 1:7–8 has Gaza, Ashdod, Ashkelon, Ekron; Jer 25:20 has Ashkelon, Gaza, Ekron, Ashdod; and Zech 9:5–6, like Jer 25:20, has Ashkelon, Gaza, Ekron, Ashdod. This suggests that the list of four, although not their order, had become formulaic, either for literary and/or geopolitical reasons. Ball suggests that Gath did not exist at the time of Zephaniah. (But this would not explain its absence from Amos 1:7–8, for it is mentioned in Amos 6:2.) Roberts feels that Gath was omitted in our verse because it was under Judean control. Haak, who has reviewed the archaeological evidence pertaining to all of these cities, concludes that Gath was not under Judean control but was omitted because it ceased to be important after its destruction in the eighth century. Cf. Paul, 17 and 56, for Gath's omission in Amos 1:7–8.

According to Assyrian sources these four Philistine cities were given parts of Judean territory by Sennacherib (see Cogan, p. 66, note 12).

The choice of the cities may have been due more to poetic reasons than to geopolitical ones. Four is a symmetrical number that lends itself to poetic parallelism of two matching pairs. In fact, the pairing of these cities is always chiastic, based on their initial letters, *ʾalep* (Ashkelon, Ashdod) or *ʿayin* (Gaza [*ʿazza*], Ekron). Gath, beginning with *gimmel*, has no sound pair (DNF).

Ky, "for," which begins this verse, has been taken by many as an emphatic ("indeed") rather than a conjunction, because they do not join v. 4 with v. 3 but view it as the beginning of the next section. I see no reason to do this since I take this verse to be part of the "Last Chance to Repent" section and not part of the "Prophecy Against the Nations" (see COMMENT for further discussion). The impending disaster announced in 2:4 provides the motivation, urged in 2:3, for the people to seek the Lord (Sweeney, 397).

Actually, v. 4 may serve as a bridge between two sections, belonging in some ways to both. It is joined to the preceding section by *ky*, and separated from the following one by virtue of the fact that *hwy* in v. 5 begins a new section (cf. 3:1). But v. 4 enumerates Philistine cities, and that is the location of the first in the series of destructions that follows.

Zephaniah's use of the Day of the Lord in 2:3–4 is presumably in accord with his use of this concept in Chapter 1 (see NOTE to 1:7). Both Ezek 30:2–3 and Obad 15 express the view that this day will bring catastrophe to the nations. It may first serve as a warning to Israel/Judah, and then, after they have suffered destruction, a warning to other nations that the same fate awaits them, after which Israel will be restored.

At noon they will drive her out. The inhabitants will be driven out of the city. "At noon" seems to mean "suddenly" in Jer 15:8, and presumably has the same connotation here. Ball follows Smith in suggesting that the city will be taken quickly; the battle begun at daybreak (the usual time for an assault) will be over by noon. Christensen (678) implies that this may be a contrast to the lengthy siege of Ashdod by Psammetichus I, said by Herodotus (2.157) to have lasted twenty-nine years. Once again, scholars may be too eager to read historical reality into poetic soundplay. The *š* sound echoes in the Ashkelon-Ashdod clauses.

On the other hand, other scholars have attempted to improve the soundplay by making this phrase more consonant, in line with the soundplay in the rest of the verse. Thomas (*ET* 74) suggests that there is a root *šdd*, meaning "drive away" (cf. Prov 19:26), and that there is a semantic play on the *meaning* of "Ashdod" (*šdd*) and *grš*, "drive out," although not a soundplay on their phonemes. Zalcman (*VT* 36) says that the prophet was more concerned with expressing a double entendre than with simple assonance (see COMMENT for his complete analysis). He points to Jer 15:8 and Ps 91:6 (as did several medieval Jewish commentators), both of which contain *šdd bṣhrym*, "ravage/destroy at noon." Zalcman suggests that this reflects a known expression which would readily be evoked by the listener/reader of our verse. Hence the wordplay is not expressed directly within our verse, but is transferred to it by the listener who supplies the missing link, the known expression.

COMMENT

The time of punishment is imminent, the day of the wrath of the Lord draws swiftly near, and the people of Judah can withstand the heat of his fury no better than a bundle of straw. But the "humble of the land," the poorer classes (as opposed to the wealthy mentioned in 1:8–13) or those loyal to God, are urged to seek safety from the destruction. If they will seek the Lord (which those mentioned in 1:6 failed to do), perhaps they will escape the disaster. The totality and finality of the prophecy of destruction is moderated by a ray of last-minute hope. There is, perhaps, a call to repent implicit in these verses, or perhaps it is just encouragement for the faithful. For there is no absolute guarantee of escape, only the possibility. (See Hunter, 259–71, for a discussion of this section in conjunction with other prophetic exhortations. Cf. also Swee-ney, *CBQ* 53, 397–99.)

There is no consensus on whether to construe 2:4 with the preceding verses or the following ones. I follow the scribal division in the MT (in this case but not always) and note that some modern translations (NEB, NRSV) have also adopted this division. Many scholars prefer to keep all the references to Philistia in one section, and therefore segment vv. 1–3 and 4–15. But this causes problems; as Roberts notes, the prophecy against Philistia begins abruptly and then is followed by a *hoy* oracle. Roberts solves the problem by reversing the order of vv. 4 and 5, which are then separated from vv. 1–3. But I see no reason that all mention of the Philistines necessarily belongs to one pericope. On the contrary, the mention of the Philistines at the end of one and the beginning of another forms a nice seam (whether or not these were once separate oracles or merely subdivisions in one discourse). This allows *hoy* to stand at the beginning of its oracle, where one would expect it. It also eliminates the problem of *ki* which is difficult to construe as a conjunction if it opens a section but makes good sense if one takes it as the conclusion of a description of the Day of the Lord in which doom for Philistia is part of the scenario.

A literary interpretation also supports the division of vv. 1–4 and 5–15, for the image of Philistia in v. 4 is quite different from that in vv. 5–7. The later passage, which equates Philistia with Canaan, is part of a larger unit which evokes a more ancient view of the world's nations (see COMMENT to the following section). The image of v. 4, as analyzed by L. Zalcman (*VT* 36) and modified by R. Gordis (*VT* 37), is taken from a different sphere of life altogether. The cities, as Zalcman has perceptively shown, are personified as women and consigned to four bitter fates associated with women: abandonment, spinsterhood (Gordis amends this to desertion), divorce, and barrenness. The verbs chosen in each case can be applied equally well to a city and to a woman's status. For *ʿzwbh* cf. Isa 54:6; Jer 4:29; for *šmmh* cf. Isa 54:1; 2 Sam 13:20; for *grš* cf. Lev 21:14; *ʿqr* is the same root used for barrenness, e.g., Isa 54:1. This, according to Zalcman, is the reason that *grš* was used instead of *šdd*. For while *šdd* can be applied to humans, it is gender-neutral, but *grš* is specifically used for a divorced woman. Gordis, accepting Zalcman's interpretation with a slight modification, sees here an ascending scale of suffering associated with women: Gaza will be deserted like a betrothed woman deserted by her fiancé, Ashkelon will be desolate like a wife abandoned by her husband, Ashdod will be driven out like a divorced woman, and Ekron will be uprooted like a barren woman.

The metaphor of the wife, in all of its permutations, is common in the prophets when applied to Israel (cf. Isaiah 54), but novel when applied to Philistia. However, the implication is that the same fate will be shared by Judah if she cannot escape on the day of the wrath of the Lord.

V. Prophecy Against the Nations (2:5–15)

♦

⁵Woe, inhabitants of the seacoast, nation of Cherethites.
The word of the Lord is against you, Canaan, land of the
      Philistines:
I will destroy you, make you uninhabitable.
⁶The seacoast shall be encampments of shepherds' pastures and
      sheepfolds.
⁷It shall be a portion for the remnant of the House of Judah
On which they shall graze;
In the houses of Ashkelon at evening they shall lie down.
For the Lord their God will attend to them and will restore their
      fortunes.
⁸I have heard the taunts of Moab,
And the insults of the Ammonites,
Who have taunted my people,
And made boasts over their territory.
⁹Therefore, by my life, says the Lord of Hosts, God of Israel,
Moab shall be like Sodom,
And the Ammonites like Gomorrah—
Clumps of weeds and patches of salt, a permanent wasteland.
The remnant of my people will plunder them,
And the remainder of my nation shall possess them.
¹⁰This is what they get for their pride,
For they taunted and boasted against the people of the Lord of
      Hosts.

¹¹The Lord is awesome against them,
For he shrivels all the gods of the land.
To him will bow, each from its place,
All the islands of the nations.
¹²Moreover, it is you, Cushites, who are the ones slain by my
sword.
¹³And let him stretch his hand against the north and destroy
Ashur,
And let him make Nineveh a desolation, arid as the desert.
¹⁴In it herds shall lie down, every nation's beasts.
Both the jackdaw and the owl shall roost on its capitals,
A voice shall shriek from the window—a raven at the sill,
For its cedarwork is stripped bare.
¹⁵This is the joyful city, dwelling secure,
Telling itself: I am the one and only.
Alas, she has become a desolation, a lair of wild animals.
Anyone who passes by hisses, shakes his hand.

NOTES

5. *Woe.* *Hoy* (but not ʾoy) is particular to prophets. The one occurrence outside of the classical prophets, 1 Kgs 13:30, is uttered by a prophet. Possibly originating as a lament for the dead, *hoy* comes to take on the sense of an invective, a threat of doom, or a condemnation. Against this, however, some scholars (e.g., Roberts, 114, 118) are of the opinion that *hoy* may be a simple exclamation or vocative particle whose function is to get the attention of the hearer (it is generally followed by direct address), like English "hey." Roberts feels that the overtones of doom come from the context, not the basic meaning of the word. There is a tendency for *hoy* discourse to occur in series, as in Zeph 2:5 and 3:1. (See *TDOT* III, 359–64; Andersen and Freedman, *Amos*, 520; and Hillers, "*Hoy* and *Hoy*-Oracles: A Neglected Syntactic Aspect.")

Nation of Cherethites. Peoples of Crete, a designation for the Philistines. The Cherethites are elsewhere associated with the Philistines (Ezek 25:16 and cf. 1 Sam 30:14), since Philistine origins are in the

Mediterranean islands. Ben Zvi finds a wordplay in *krtym*, "Cherethites," and *krt*, "cut off" (cf. Ezek 25:16). Cf. also Zeph 2:6, *nwt krt*.

Canaan, land of the Philistines. "Canaan" is the designation for the area in Palestine-Syria under Egyptian control during the fourteenth to thirteenth centuries B.C.E., and, of course, for the land promised to the Israelites in the Bible. Its western and eastern borders are described in Gen 10:19: "The Canaanite territory extended from Sidon in the direction of Gerar, as far as Gaza, and in the direction of Sodom, Gomorrah, Admah, and Zeboim, as far as Lasha" and in Num 13:29: "Canaanites dwell by the Sea and along the Jordan." Canaan is the broader designation of which Philistia forms a part—cf. Josh 13:2–3: "All the districts of the Philistines and all the Geshurites . . . are accounted Canaanite." "Philistia" (*ʾrṣ plštym*) refers more specifically to the southern coastal plain, cf. Gen 21:32, 34; Exod 13:17; 1 Sam 27:1; 29:1; 1 Kgs 5:1.

Linguistically, the construction is two terms in apposition. There is no need, however, for them to be exactly synonymous; rather, this is a case of the kind of association of a whole and its part, like "Judah and Jerusalem," common in parallelistic discourse. The construction "Canaan, land of the Philistines" is similar to "Babylonia, land of the Chaldeans" in Jer 50:1, 45; Ezek 12:13.

Although "Canaan" can be used to refer to Philistia, the term "Canaan" is rarely found after the Book of Judges. By and large it occurs in accounts of the pre-settlement and settlement periods, in Genesis–Judges, and a few times in later literature when referring to this period. It is used in Isa 23:11 and 2 Sam 24:7 to refer to Phoenicia, in 1 Kgs 9:16 for the inhabitants of Gezer, and in several other verses in the sense of "merchants" (cf. Zeph 1:11). It is an archaic term and is never used during the monarchic period to refer to contemporary Philistines. Why, then, has Zephaniah used it here? Because, as the COMMENT will explain, he wants to recall Gen 10:19 and the view that Philistia is part of Canaan.

NEB renders "Canaan" as "I will subdue you," taking it from the root *knʿ*, but there is little to recommend this.

6. The territory once populated by Philistines will become pasturelands. The verse is syntactically and lexically problematic.

The verb *hyth*, "shall become," is feminine, although the apparent subject, *hbl hym*, is masculine. Probably "land of the Philistines," which is feminine, is the implied subject; it is the last-mentioned antecedent and its feminine gender is evident in "I will destroy you [fem. sing.]." Perhaps *hbl hym* crept in from the preceding or the following verse. LXX omits it in v. 6, translating the full expression in v. 7 instead of MT's *hbl*.

Encampments of shepherds' pastures. This phrase is difficult, as witnessed by the variety offered in the Ancient Versions and modern translations. *Krt* may be a dittography from the previous verse. NJPS and NEB, following LXX, understand *krt* to refer to the Cherethites. It has been analyzed as a defective form of *krᶜt*, from the root *rᶜh*, "to pasture," by Ehrlich; but is more likely to be from *kr*, "pasture" (cf. Isa 30:23). Bolle suggests that the construction be understood as "the abode of the shepherds and their pasture," on the analogy of Isa 11:2: "a spirit of devotion and reverence for the Lord" and Ezek 31:16: "the choicest and best of Lebanon." Roberts and others reverse the order of *krt* and *nwt*. I have kept the order of the MT and understood the phrase as a construct chain. Such a construction is unusual but not impossible (cf. Gen 41:10; 47:9). Ben Zvi prefers to see this as either a conflation of two traditional variants or as *krt rᶜym* and its gloss, *nwt*.

The unusual *krt* has led to more fanciful interpretations, e.g., "cisterns," based on *krh*, "to dig wells" (cf. Gen 26:25; Num 21:18—so Ibn Caspi, Segal, and Mandelkern; or "meal, feast," based on 2 Kgs 6:23 (so Rashi, Malbim).

The spelling of *newot* also presents some difficulty. The phrase *neʾot roᶜim* appears in Amos 1:2; in Jer 33:12 we find *neweh roᶜim*. Zeph 2:6 seems to have a combination of these two spellings, found nowhere else, and adding to the impression that the text is defective here. Note that Jer 33:12 conveys much the same picture as our passage. (For an excellent literary analysis of the phrase in Amos 1:2 see Weiss, *The Bible from Within*, 208–16.)

7. *Portion.* The word *hbl* has a double meaning: it may be understood as a shortened form of *hbl hym*, "seacoast," and as "portion, inheritance." Thus the phrase also means "The coast shall belong to the remnant of the House of Judah."

On which. I follow the NRSV in taking this as a relative clause with the relative pronoun not expressed, as this most closely reflects the masoretic accents. It is also possible to take it as an independent clause, parallel to the following one, as most translations do. The Hebrew is *ᶜlyhm*, "on them." The antecedent of "them" is unclear but is most likely the encampments of v. 6. That this would yield a masculine suffix referring to a feminine antecedent is not an insurmountable problem— cf. Exod 15:20–21. (For other cases of lack of concord in gender see Waltke and O'Connor, 109–10.)

Smith and others emend to *ᶜl hym*, "by the sea." Roberts accepts "by the sea" and adds "in the daytime," restoring *yomam*, a parallel to "in the evening," which he feels was lost by haplography after *hayyam*, "the sea." J. Kselman (*CBQ* 32) has suggested the reading *ᶜulehem*, "their nurslings," but this has not been widely accepted.

In the houses of Ashkelon. The abandoned homes of the Philistines will serve as barns for Judean flocks. (See below.) The repetition of "house" in "the House of Judah" and "the houses of Ashkelon" underlines the contrast between the two peoples.

At evening. A nice parallel to "at noon" in v. 4.

They shall graze . . . they shall lie down. The syntax of this verse has elicited much comment. The plural subjects of these verbs seem to refer to the remnant of the House of Judah (the only apparent antecedent), a collective singular. A singular collective can govern a plural verb, as in 2:1 (see Waltke and O'Connor, 113). The verb *rᶜh*, "to graze, pasture," may be used of shepherds or of sheep; *rbṣ*, "to lie down," is normally used of animals, not of humans. Exceptions are Job 11:19 and Zeph 3:13, and several metaphoric usages in which humans are compared to animals (Ps 23:2; Isa 14:30; Ezek 34:14). Here, too, the usage may be metaphoric: the remnant of the House of Judah, like a flock, will graze and bed down in what once were the cities of Philistia.

Most interpreters do not take this verse quite so metaphorically. Some view the subjects of the verbs as Judean shepherds, who will graze their sheep and find lodging (NEB, NRSV, NJPS, Ball, Roberts). This means that *rbṣ* applies to humans in a non-metaphoric way. Perhaps this term was employed because it often forms a word pair with *rᶜh*. NJPS suggests a possible emendation from the *qal* to the *hip'il*, yielding "they [the shepherds] shall bed down [their flocks]."

Others view the subject as real sheep who will graze and rest (LXX, KJV, Bolle). LXX adds "from before the children of Judah" after "they shall lie down," thereby making clear that it took the subject of the verb to be the flocks and not the House of Judah.

A final possibility is to view the subjects of *r'h* and *rbṣ* as echoes of the last terms in v. 6: shepherds and flocks. (We have already had to look back to v. 6 for the antecedent of "on them," so it seems permissible to do so again here.) The two verbs, *r'h* and *rbṣ*, would then have two different subjects, "shepherd" and "flocks," which would form an ABAB parallelism. This rendering preserves the rhetorically superior image of having the Philistine houses occupied by Judean livestock.

Verses 7a and 7d also form a continuity concerning Judah, with 7c providing a contrast with the Philistines. There is, then, point and counterpoint between the idea of what will happen to the Philistine territory and God's care of Judah.

Some of the intricate relationships in vv. 6–7 can be diagrammed as follows:

seacoast *(ḥbl hym)*
    pasture for shepherds
    folds for flocks
portion *(ḥbl)*
    House of Judah
        they shall graze
    houses of Ashkelon
        they shall lie down
    attend to them [= Judah]

The Lord their God. The prophet addresses the Philistines in his own voice, referring to God in the third person. Or, alternatively, God refers to himself in the third person (Roberts). This is one of many switches from first to third person in this book.

8. The next group of nations to be doomed are Judah's neighbors to the east, Moab and Ammon. The precise historical reference is unclear,

but it is likely that there were periodic confrontations over territory between these nations and Judah. Christensen identifies this reference with the events of 650–640 B.C.E. when Kamashalta, king of Moab, regained hegemony in Transjordan, only to be subsequently weakened by Arab incursions and Josiah's territorial expansion. But the reference need not be to a specific instance. See COMMENT for further discussion. Moab and Ammon are often singled out for especially negative notice—cf. Gen 19:37–38 and Deut 23:4.

Ammonites. Hebrew: *bny ʿmwn,* "sons of Ammon." This is a conventional way of referring to Ammon, cf. Gen 19:38; Jer 9:25; 25:21; 27:3.

Made boasts. Hebrew *ygdylw ʿl,* or the longer form of the idiom *hgdyl ph ʿl,* literally "to make great the mouth over" or "to gloat," occurs in Jer 48:26, 42 (in connection with Moab); Ezek 35:13; Obad 12; Ps 35:26; 38:17; 41:10; 55:13; Job 19:5. As in our verse, it is often found in association with *hrp.* An alternative interpretation is "enlarged their territory." Whether this refers to the actual seizure of land, and, if so, whether it occurred close to the time of this prophecy, is unclear. Compare Jer 49:1.

9. *Sodom . . . Gomorrah.* An image of total destruction aptly applied to Moab and Ammon since these nations were incestuously conceived when Lot fled from Sodom (Gen 19:37–38).

Clumps of weeds and patches of salt. The exact meaning of these terms is difficult to ascertain, since *mmšq* and *mkrh* are *hapax legomena* and *hrwl* is rare. See Greenfield. The Versions struggled with this phrase, all producing different translations, showing that this is an ancient crux. The gist is that the area, which is near the Dead Sea, will be covered with weeds and salt deposits—that is, it will become permanently infertile. Compare the curse in Deut 29:23, which also contains the idea of salinized, infertile soil and destruction likened to Sodom and its neighboring towns. Cf. also Jer 48:9.

Clumps. Hebrew *mmšq* has been related to *mšk,* "to draw along, to acquire." LXX equates it with Damascus, *dmšq,* apparently under the influence of Gen 15:2. Targum reads *mšmt,* which Greenfield explains as based on reading the Hebrew as *mimsaq,* from a root which in Mishnaic Hebrew means "to pluck, pull olives." Hence, "a place for harvesting nettles."

Weeds. The word *ḥrwl* occurs in Job 30:7 and Prov 24:31. It is a type of weed, which, from these contexts, grows tall and has thick foliage. Weeds or nettles are the antithesis of useful agricultural products.

Patches. Hebrew *mkrh* is often derived from the root *krh*, "to dig" (so Targum), hence "salt pits." Others connect it with an Akkadian, Aramaic, and Syriac word for "heap" (so LXX and Vulgate). Greenfield renders "a place for mining salt"—i.e., salt pits.

My nation. So the *qere.* The *ketiv* omits the possessive suffix. Either is acceptable. Perhaps the fact that the next word starts with *y*- influenced this writing. If *qere* reflects a more accurate spelling, there would have been three *yods* in a row.

10. This verse recapitulates v. 8. LXX omits "the people."

11. *Awesome.* God's power will instill fear and awe in Moab and Ammon. For a discussion of the awe-inspiring nature of God see Roberts, 201–2 with references. Hebrew *nwrʾ*, "awe-inspiring," is from the root *yrʾ* (cf. Ps 96:4 and 1 Chr 16:25); but LXX and Peshitta take it from *rʾh*, translating "will appear." As it does elsewhere (e.g., Gen 1:1), NEB adopts both readings: "The Lord will appear against them with all his terrors."

Against them. "Or "over them."

For. Hebrew *ky* may also be understood as an emphatic, "indeed." (So Ball, Roberts, and others; cf. Muraoka, 158–64.) LXX and Vulgate omit it, as do several modern translations. NJPS gives it its full cause-and-effect force: "Causing all the gods on earth to shrivel."

Shrivels. Hebrew *rzh* is in the *qal* perfect and is usually taken from the root meaning "to be thin." The verb in the *qal* occurs only here and its use is puzzling. Roberts would prefer a *piʿel* imperfect. LXX and Peshitta translate "destroy" although it is not clear how they arrived at this, other than from the general context. In Aramaic the root *rzh* means "to be strong, hard." Cf. *razon*, "prince," in Prov 14:28. Thus Sabottka proposes "to rule, control."

The idea seems to be that the Lord will constrict or shrink the foreign gods by constricting the land over which they have dominion. The diminution of these gods will demonstrate the superiority of the Lord. Robertson puts it more concretely: when the territories of Moab and

Ammon are devastated, they will produce no food, and their gods will become thin and starve.

Each from its place. Roberts views this as universal acknowledgment of the Lord, as in Isa 19:19–25 and Mal 1:14; and distinguishes this from the "Zion tradition" of Isa 2:2–4; Mic 4:1–4; and Zech 14:16–19 in which all the nations will stream to the Temple in Jerusalem to worship the Lord. But see the following NOTE. O'Connor, *HVS*, 253, renders "from his own temple," connecting *maqom* with Arabic *maqam*, "holy place, shrine."

Islands of the nations. This is often viewed as a general designation for far-flung peoples (cf. Isaiah 42:10 and *passim*). But the precise term "islands of the nations" is found only here and in Gen 10:5, where it refers to an offshoot of the descendants of Japheth, the nations of Anatolia and the Aegean. (See B. Oded, "The Table of Nations [Genesis 10]—a Socio-cultural Approach," ZAW 98 [1986], esp. p. 29.)

I understand the term to refer to the descendants of Japheth, with perhaps, if we seek a more specific historical correlation, a nod to the Medes, Cimmerians, and Scythians (cf. Madai, Gomer, and Ashkenaz in Gen 10:2–3 and see COMMENT). Thus the picture is not one of universal acknowledgment of the Lord, but acknowledgment by the islands of the nations when they witness the Lord's judgment against Moab and Ammon.

12. *Moreover.* For *gam* as an emphatic, in addition to its additive force, see Muraoka, 143–46, and Andersen, *The Sentence in Biblical Hebrew*, 155–67. The use here suggests Cushites in addition to those already mentioned, and *even* Cushites, i.e., those who might have expected to be exempt from God's power.

Cushites. This verse is abrupt, giving little space to this group of people, whose identity is unclear. Furthermore, one might have expected "Cush" rather than "Cushites." There are five possible interpretations of "Cushites."

(1) *Egypt.* Most scholars translate "Ethiopians," which they equate with Egypt, as the two lands are geographically adjacent and sometimes occur in parallelism. But, it should be noted, while Cush occurs together with Egypt, it never stands in place of Egypt. Some scholars get around this by explaining that the reference is to the Ethiopian pharaohs who

had ruled Egypt before Psammetichus I. Others see here a reference to Ethiopians who served in the Egyptian army and who are mentioned in connection with the battle at Karkemish in 605 (Jer 46:8–9). All are bothered by the omission of Egypt—a major world power whose name would be expected in this list. But one wonders why the prophet did not simply come out and say "Egyptians" if that is what he meant. He was not reluctant to mention Assyria and the other nations by name.

(2) *Ethiopia or Nubia.* Ball, 141, accepts the identification with Ethiopia proper (as opposed to Ethiopia as a substitute for Egypt). He suggests that the reference is to distant, exotic lands to the south which, like the islands of the nations (which he takes in a general sense of "all the lands of the nations"), will feel the power of the Lord. Ball, like others, likes the geographic symmetry (west = Philistia, east = Moab and Ammon, south = Ethiopia, north = Assyria) that this interpretation provides.

(3) *Midian, or tribes to the south of Judah.* R. Haak notes that "Cush" or "Cushan" may refer to Midian or another tribe in the area south of Judah (cf. Hab 3:7; Num 12:1; and perhaps 2 Chr 21:16; and see Eph'al, 78). This would mean that 2:12 is an afterthought tacked on to the fate of Moab and Ammon, mentioning another people in the same general area. But Midian is not usually listed among the enemies of Judah at this time; it is rather Edom that one expects. Yet Edom is absent, and it stretches credibility to find in "Cushites" a reference to Edom.

(4) *Tribes of the Arabian peninsula.* Gen 10:7 lists the sons of Cush, peoples located in northern (or perhaps southern) Arabia (see Eph'al, 227–29). But this hardly seems relevant to Zephaniah.

(5) *Mesopotamia, or, more specifically, Assyria.* The same Cush of Gen 10:7 is also the father of Nimrod, the builder of Assyria. I prefer this interpretation because in Zeph 3:10 there is an even stronger possibility that "Cush" refers to Mesopotamia, and because the order of certain terms in our passage—"Cushites" following "the islands of the nations" and then followed by "Ashur" and "Nineveh"—reinforces my feeling that we have here an allusion to Gen 10:5–11, where the same terms occur (along with some others) in the same order. In Gen 10:5 we find "the islands of the nations." Then Gen 10:6 moves to the sons of Ham,

the first of which is Cush. "Cush," according to Speiser (*Genesis*, 66), is used to designate two widely separate lands: Ethiopia and the land of the Kassites (Akkadian *kuššu*; Greek *Kossaios*). Speiser interprets Gen 10:6 as the former; but 10:8, in which the genealogy of Cush culminates in the birth of Nimrod, who gave rise to the kingdoms of Mesopotamia whence came Ashur and Nineveh, refers to the latter. I assume that Zephaniah, not having read Speiser, did not distinguish the two meanings of "Cush." For him the brother of Egypt, Put, and Canaan and the father of Nimrod were one and the same. In any case, all are descendants of Ham. In the context of vv. 13–15, "Cushites," therefore, signifies not the military-political complex of Egypt, but the descendants of the forebearer of the Assyrian empire (which derives from the line of Ham). See COMMENT for further discussion.

Perhaps there is support for this identification in Ps 87:5, which mentions Rahab (= Egypt) and Babylonia, followed by Philistia and Tyre with Cush. Although most commentaries link Cush (= Ethiopia) with Rahab, it is possible to see here an ABAB pattern: Rahab (= Egypt) and Babylonia; and the domains associated with Egyptian control—Philistia and Tyre; and the domain associated with Babylonia—Cush.

Who are the ones slain by my sword. A few emend *ḥrby* to *ḥrb y* (an abbreviation for the tetragrammaton), "the sword of the Lord." This keeps the reference to God in the third person (O'Connor, Ben Zvi). But we have already found numerous shifts from the prophet's speech to God's speech.

The syntax, while unusual, is explainable, although that does not entirely remove the difficulties in understanding this verse. The Hebrew contains a verbless sentence with pleonastic pronoun serving as copula. The pleonastic pronoun, *hmh*, is in the third person plural, while the subject, also a pronoun, is in the second person plural. For constructions with pleonastic pronouns see Muraoka, 67–76; Waltke and O'Connor, 298; and Geller. An example resembling our verse, with second person subject and third person pleonastic pronoun, is Ezek 22:24, *ʾat ʾereṣ loʾ meṭohara hiʾ*. (What follows in Ezekiel 22 is echoed in Zephaniah 3.) Other examples are 2 Sam 7:28 and Ps 44:5. In fact, Muraoka, 71, observes that in biblical Hebrew there are no examples of a pronominal copula in first or second person.

Geller equates the pleonastic construction with English cleft sentences (hence my translation). All of the grammatical discussions agree that this construction contains emphasis. The word *gam* is also emphatic, so there is double emphasis in the verse. Exactly what is being emphasized, however, remains elusive. It would seem that the syntax of this verse directs attention to a new topic, the Cushites (the subject), and emphasizes that they are the ones slain by God's sword (the predicate). Geller finds that cleft sentences highlight a relational aspect in connected speech. While the exact nuance of this relational aspect varies with the context, the largest category of nuances involves contrastive emphasis. Perhaps the method of the Cushites' destruction is being contrasted to the vaguer methods mentioned in connection with the other nations. In the end, the problem with this verse is not its internal syntax, but its relationship to the surrounding discourse.

13. The passage about Assyria is framed by the stretching out of God's hand against it in v. 13 and the shaking of the passerby's hand in derision in v. 15. Like the cities of Philistia, the great urban centers of Assyria will become depopulated and abandoned, a pastureland for herds and a nesting place for wild birds. The stretching of God's hand occurs also in 1:4, where it is aimed against Judah. For a discussion of this idiom see Humbert, *VT* 12.

Let him stretch. The verbs in this verse are jussives. The use of the jussive here may be rhetorical, conveying a "distinctive pragmatic force" (Waltke and O'Connor, 568) or "to vary verb sequences and literary texture" (570).

Ashur. This may be the city Ashur (a former capital of Assyria) or the country of Assyria. It is more likely the latter, since countries are the subject of this prophecy.

Arid as the desert. The image is a common one, cf. Jer 50:12; 51:43. Olivier suggests, however, that *ṣyh* may mean "wild animals" instead of "arid." He bases this on Isa 13:21; 23:13; 34:14 and the various animals mentioned in vv. 14–15. Our phrase would then mean "wild animals/demons of the desert." Olivier also notes the similarity to the curses in ancient near eastern treaties and Deuteronomy.

14. *Every nation's beasts.* Hebrew *kl ḥytw gwy* is unusual. More common is "beasts of the land" (Gen 1:24; Ps 79:2), "beasts of the field"

114

(Ps 104:11; cf. Isa 56:9), or "beasts of the forest" (Ps 50:10; 104:20). LXX reads "of the land" in place of "of a nation." The Targum has "all the beasts of the field." Many emend, following the LXX and the Targum. Preserving gwy, however, preserves a play on the same word in v. 11. Ball, 110, noting the parallelism between "land/earth" and "nation" in v. 11, suggests seeing both meanings inherent in our phrase. There is also a certain irony in the picture of Assyria being overrun by other nations' wildlife, even as Assyria overran and gained control of many of its neighbors.

Jackdaw. The identification of this and the following animal is disputed. Q'>t is an unclean bird (Lev 11:18; Deut 14:17). Ps 102:7 associates it with the steppe or desert. LXX translates "chameleon"; Vulgate and Targum have "pelican."

Owl. The Versions translate "hedgehog, porcupine" (cf. Isa 14:23; 34:11. Note that the two difficult terms q'>t and qpd both occur in Isa 34:11). Modern scholars prefer to see here a type of wild bird, given that the term is found in the context of other birds nesting in the tops of the columns. But Roberts notes that the columns would be lying on the ground and therefore any animal could make a home in their capitals. However, the point is not that the buildings lie in ruins, but that they are harboring animals.

Capitals. According to Paul, 274–75, the capitals of the Temple in Amos 9:1 are "the spherical knobs at the heads of the columns of the pillars." Nineveh is symbolized by its temple or palace—a grand structure now used only as a roost.

A voice shall shriek from the window. Many modern translations, continuing the list of birds from the previous phrase, render this phrase as "The great owl shall hoot from the window." This is based on an emendation from qwl to kws (cf. Lev 11:17; Deut 14:16; Ps 102:7). The Versions, whose rendering is closer to mine, understand the voice to belong to the birds and animals previously mentioned; I understand it to refer to the piercing call of the raven mentioned in the following phrase. The masoretic accents also join "voice . . . threshold" into one phrase. An added problem is that the root šyr/šorer is normally reserved for human beings, not birds.

A raven at the sill. I take ḥrb as meaning ʿrb, found already in LXX and Vulgate. The Targum, retaining *ḥrb*, reads "the doors have been destroyed." It is not clear whether this phrase should be linked with the previous one, as I have done, or with the following, as done by the Targum and Ball. Ehrlich makes the novel suggestion to understand the meaning as "the sound [of the wind blowing] through the window, a hole [reading *ḥr* for *ḥrb*, with dittography of the *b*] in the door." O'Connor, *HVS*, 254, reads *ḥereb*, "sword," for *ḥoreb*, along with Aquila, Symmachus, and Sabottka. Also to be considered is Ben Zvi's suggestion; he retains the MT *ḥoreb*, which he renders "desolation," as in Isa 61:4 and Jer 49:13.

Sill. For *sp*, which usually means "threshold, doorjamb," see Paul, 275 note 18. He also notes that "capital and threshold/doorjamb" is a merismus for the entire structure, from top to bottom. In our verse it is better to understand *sp* as the window frame or sill. Cf. Ezek 41:16 (albeit a confusing verse) for "*spym* and windows" and also note that they are paneled.

For its cedarwork is stripped bare. Presumably the decorative wood paneling has been stripped off by the birds. The noun lacks a *mappiq*, if it indeed means "its cedarwork." Or perhaps it is just a feminine collective noun (cf. *ʿṣh* from *ʿṣ* in Jer 6:6). The verb has been analyzed as a third-person masculine singular *piʿel*, meaning "he [a bird?] stripped." The Versions seem at a loss to render this phrase exactly. For another possibility see Sabottka.

The description of Assyria is more elaborate not only because we are reaching the climax of the prophecy, but because Assyrian cities and buildings were, indeed, more elaborate than anything that Philistia or Moab had to offer. Our verse reflects the reality of Assyrian palaces, with an ironic twist. They did contain beams and paneling of cedar and other types of wood; and, in addition to the huge statues of winged bulls and lions, and the ever-present reliefs of victorious campaigns, there were, especially in the time of Ashurbanipal when this art form reached its peak, reliefs of hunting scenes depicting many animals (Lloyd, 204, 212). It is as if Zephaniah is playing on the artistic menagerie in Assyrian palaces and turning it into a vision of destruction and ruin.

15. The prophet mocks Nineveh's false sense of security and utters a lament, to be understood ironically, over its fate. For similar phraseology

see Isa 47:7–8 and Ezek 25:5. While highly formulaic, the verse is a nice summation of the preceding verses.

This is the joyful city. Many commentators read this as an unmarked interrogative, "Is this the joyful city?" similar to 2 Sam 16:17: "Is this your loyalty to your friend?" The implication is the same, whether or not the interrogative is marked: the true condition of the city is the opposite of the expected one. Compare Isa 23:7; Lam 2:15; Ruth 1:19.

Joyful. This adjective is used in Isa 22:2; 23:7; 24:8; 32:13; Zeph 3:11—all describing exulting ones soon to be destroyed (Ball). For similar phraseology see Isa 47:8.

Alas. Hebrew *ʾyk*, like *ʾykh*, "how," often indicates lamentation discourse. Cf. 2 Sam 1:19; Isa 14:12; Ps 73:19; and Isa 1:21; Lam 1:1.

Who passes by. This is a common literary figure for presenting an external view of a destruction. Cf. Isa 34:10; 60:15; Jer 9:9, 11; 18:16; 19:8; 49:17; 50:13; Ezek 5:14; 14:15; 16:15; 33:28; 35:7; 36:34; Zeph 3:6; Lam 2:15; 2 Chr 7:21. Worse than a passerby viewing the destruction is the absence of a passerby altogether, as in, for example, Isa 60:15.

Hisses, shakes his hand. Gestures of derision. For hissing and shaking the head see Jer 18:16; 50:13, and *passim*; Lam 2:15. Shaking the hand is unusual. DNF suggests that while shaking the head reinforces the derision, shaking the hand adds a threatening gesture, as if to imply physical harm.

COMMENT

Zephaniah's prophecy against the nations, like those found in other prophetic books (e.g., Isaiah, Jeremiah, Ezekiel, Amos, Joel, and others), is not to be understood as literally directed to those nations. Rather, the audience for this prophecy is Judah. In general, such prophecies serve to emphasize the universal power of God and his control over all parts of the world, including hostile lands. More specifically, these prophecies may serve different rhetorical functions. For example, in Amos 1–2 the announcement of the destruction of the other nations precedes the announcement against Judah and Israel. One can imagine the Israelite audience initially agreeing with Amos—even cheering him on—for surely Damascus and the rest deserve the worst that God could bring upon them. But then, caught in the rhetorical trap, they must likewise agree that Judah, and in the case of Amos, Israel, also deserve God's punishment. Israel has behaved no better, and will fare no better, than its enemies.

The rhetorical situation in Zephaniah 2 is somewhat different. The MT's placement of the destruction of the nations after the destruction of Judah announced in Chapter 1 leads to the perception that the destruction of the nations is an aftereffect of the destruction of Judah. It has therefore been interpreted by traditional Jewish commentators as the preparation for the return to Judah in the postexilic period. On the other hand, it precedes the announcement of the destruction of Jerusalem in Chapter 3, making it a precursor to a yet more catastrophic destruction. Sweeney (*CBQ* 53) therefore sees in it a warning of what will happen and a call to return to the ways of the Lord. These two views can be harmonized by understanding the Day of the Lord as including the destruction of both Judah and the other nations (see NOTE to 1:7 and 2:4). The concept of the Day of the Lord is, then, both negative and positive in respect to Judah, containing elements of doom and hope. The entire Book of Zephaniah is, in that sense, a prophecy about the Day of the Lord.

Since a number of prophetic books contain prophecies against the nations (Hoffman, *JNSL* 10, finds forty or fifty), these prophecies can be considered a sub-genre or *Gattung* of prophetic writing. (For a recent summary of opinions on the origin of this *Gattung* see Paul, 7–11.) As such, they share certain literary conventions, and, like all prophetic discourse, they contain metaphoric language. But no matter how conventional the topic or how metaphoric its language, there is every reason to assume that there was a historical reality behind Zephaniah's prophecy against the nations, for a historical setting like this is not likely to have been fabricated. (However, historical accuracy does not prove that the passage was written at that very moment in history.) What, then, is the historical reality behind this prophecy? The general outline of the period of Josiah is the decline of the Assyrian empire, the growing influence of Egypt, and the rise of Babylonia. Our passage, which is clearly anti-Assyrian, would seem to refer to a time when Assyria's presence was still felt in Judah but the threat of Assyrian retaliation against a rebellious vassal was minimal. The omission of Egypt suggests that Egypt had not yet become a factor—that is, had not yet taken over Assyrian holdings on the coast. The exact date of the Egyptian takeover, and whether it was accomplished peacefully or through conquest, is not known; estimates of the date run from 633 to 618. Philistia, Moab, and Ammon were, until that time, vassals of Assyria. (Philistia then passed to Egyptian control; Moab and Ammon remained under Assyrian control until the Babylonians took over.) Zephaniah's oracle fits the overall historical picture as we know it, but gives a selective view of the world, as a rhetorical piece is apt to do. The specific details of the oracle, and its general thrust, have been interpreted in different ways.

D. Christensen (*CBQ* 46) has argued that this prophecy provides support for Josiah's program of political expansion, and that the particular nations listed are those whose territory Josiah wished to reclaim for Judah following his annexation of the northern provinces. Philistia to the west and Moab and Ammon to the east were the obstacles to Judah's territorial expansion in these directions. The taunts of Moab and Ammon in Zephaniah's oracle, according to Christensen, reflect the regained strength of these kingdoms (ca. 650–640) and their downfall suggests their weakening by Arab incursions and Josiah's expansion (ca. 628). The term "Cushites," in Christensen's view, alludes to the campaigns of Esarhaddon and Assurbanipal against the Ethiopian dynasty (Dynasty XXV) in control of Egypt, which fell in 663. He interprets 2:12 as meaning that the Assyrians cannot take credit for their victory in Egypt, for it was God's doing. Likewise, the Assyrians themselves will be defeated when God so chooses. Assyria, of course, was the major power in the area of Judah, and was in nominal control of the territories which Josiah wished to reclaim, although its control weakened noticeably from 627 on.

Although the scenario constructed by Christensen is perhaps plausible, there are too many flaws in his argument to make it convincing. First of all, there is no consensus on how much territory in the north Josiah was able to control (see Na'aman, *Tel Aviv* 18); and, moreover, it is strange, if this speech is advocating expansion, that it mentions nothing of gains in Samaria. Furthermore, the extent of Josiah's expansion to the east and west (if any) is disputed (see Oded, "Judah and the Exile," 466).

Finally, the oracles against the nations of other prophets are not interpreted as advocating territorial expansion, and there is no good reason that this one should be.

As for Christensen's explanation of the Cushites, it seems odd to refer to an incident that occurred in 663, some thirty to forty years before this prophecy. Would this piece of "ancient history," which did not directly involve Judah, really have been relevant to Zephaniah's audience?

It seems better to interpret this prophecy, as Haak ("Zephaniah's Oracles Against the Nations") does, as a generally anti-Assyrian speech without reference to territorial expansion. Assyria is the culmination of the speech, and Moab, Ammon, and the kingdoms which make up Philistia were all loyal vassals of Assyria. Zephaniah is speaking out against the great overlord Assyria and its vassals immediately adjacent to Judah. If it was composed at the time of the weakening of Assyria, this speech would have helped to revive and support Judean nationalism and stir up anti-Assyrian sentiment. Nationalism does not necessarily involve expansion; it is more a matter of promoting a sense of autonomy and national pride. That same nationalism would encourage an exilic audience to preserve and strengthen its communal identity.

This oracle may thus be seen to fit the historical context; and its general purpose may be deduced. But that does not fully explain its rhetorical shape and effect. Why has Zephaniah used terms like "Canaan," "islands of the nations," and "Cushites"? Why was Edom omitted? The answers to these questions suggest that *in addition to* historical considerations, there were traditional, cultural considerations that influenced the formation of this pericope. For meaningfulness does not reside in historical or political reality alone. Political events must be interpreted, must be seen as a part of a larger picture, must be integrated into the ongoing story of the nation. Zephaniah, I believe, does this by shaping this prophecy around an older mythopoetic theme. That theme has been preserved in literary form in Genesis 10, and it is Genesis 10, I will argue, that serves as the conceptual undergirding, and to a large extent the literary model, for Zephaniah 2:5–15. Zephaniah has taken the conventional genre *(Gattung)* of "prophecy against the nations," has tailored it to his own geopolitical reality, and has evoked an older traditional conception of the relationships among the nations of the world.

It was already pointed out in the NOTE to 2:12 that we find terminology identical with that of Genesis 10: "islands of the nations," "Cush," "Ashur," "Nineveh." We also have the equation of Philistia and Canaan, something that evokes Gen 10:19, which defines Canaan as including the entire western coast, "as far as Gaza." Moreover, Canaan also includes territory in the east, "in the direction of Sodom and Gomorrah . . ." The comparison of Moab and Ammon to Sodom and Gomorrah, while not in itself surprising (because Sodom is often used as a metaphor for destruction, and besides, there is a special connection, through Lot, between Moab and Ammon and the destruction of Sodom), nevertheless helps to draw these countries into the orbit of Canaan. Moab and Ammon have become, as it were, "eastern Canaanites." (Moab and Ammon are not mentioned in Genesis 10 and were not part of Canaan; but they must have been sufficiently important on the contemporary scene for Zephaniah to have worked them into his discourse. The point is that the prophet made the reality of his time fit the pattern in Genesis 10 by choosing the countries from Genesis 10 that were important [Philistia, Assyria], omitting those that were obscure [e.g., Put], and adding crucial ones, lacking in Genesis 10, in terminological equivalents to those in Genesis [Moab, Ammon].)

The mention of Moab and Ammon arouses the expectation that next on the list will come Edom (cf. Isa 11:14; Jer 9:25 and *passim*; Amos 1:11); yet Edom is omitted. Why? For one thing, Edom is most harshly viewed in the exilic and postexilic period (i.e., after the time of Zephaniah); and Deuteronomy, which seems to have influenced Zephaniah, treats Edom more gently than Moab and Ammon. From the historical perspective, Edom seems to have been somewhat less strongly attached to Assyria and was a growing presence in the Negev during the seventh and sixth centuries B.C.E. There was a commercial relationship between Judah and Edom, and the exact border between the two is unclear (see Bartlett and Haak, "Zephaniah's Oracles Against the Nations"). But the most compelling reason for its omission is that the Bible views Edom (= Esau) a "brother" of Jacob. Edom is genealogically too close to Israel to be considered a son of Ham; and Zephaniah's prophecy is about the sons of Ham.

Modeling his prophecy on Genesis 10, Zephaniah spoke of Assyria and its vassals bordering on Judah as if they were Canaan (Philistia, Moab, and Ammon) and Cush (Assyria). Both Canaan and Cush are the sons of Ham.

Why did Zephaniah single out the descendants of Ham? What or whom do they represent in Genesis 10 and what is their relationship to the descendants of Shem? According to the analysis of B. Oded (ZAW 98 [1986]: 14–32), which I find compelling, the Table of Nations is ordered according to a sociocultural principle. The sons of Shem represent the nomadic or semi-nomadic peoples, often shepherds; the sons of Ham represent the urban, sedentary peoples, those residing in towns or cities; and the sons of Japheth represent, by and large, the maritime peoples, residents of Anatolia and the Aegean, and also faraway nations, beyond the horizon of Shem and Ham. Oded goes on to discuss the natural antagonism between nomads and sedentary populations that anthropologists have studied, and that is expressed in the antipathy between Ham and Shem (and Japheth) in Gen 9:25–27.

The imagery in Zephaniah correlates nicely with Oded's interpretation of Genesis 10. Notice, first of all, how the urbanness of Philistia and Nineveh is stressed, in contrast to the grazing lands and animal dens that they will become. The Philistine cities will be depleted of their residents and occupied by Judean shepherds (a vivid portrayal of Israel taking possession of Canaan). Nineveh, a city *par excellence,* will be home to flocks and wildlife. Even Moab and Ammon are compared to *cities* that were destroyed. It would be difficult to picture this area near the Dead Sea as lush grazing land, so the pastureland theme is absent; but, as with the Philistines, Zephaniah has included the element of the subservience of Ham to Shem in that Israel will possess Moab and Ammon (cf. Jer 49:2).

One might demur that Zephaniah's images of destruction are quite ordinary. Certainly the prophet calls upon convention in his portrayal of the destruction of these nations: abandonment and desolation, places unfit for human settlement, mocked by passersby. But when one compares Zephaniah's imagery with the imagery in other prophecies against the nations, one notices that the others minimize the pastoral element and include more images of violent destruction. Nahum pictures the violent ravaging of Nineveh, and the breakdown of its society and culture. In Amos the Lord will send down fire to devour the foreign enemies. Jeremiah, even in his extended descriptions of attack, destruction, exile, shame, and emptiness, does not mention the coming of other people's flocks into a destroyed land.

In fact, in Zephaniah's prophecy against the nations, images of war and violence are strikingly absent, especially in contrast to his images of the destruction of Judah. He stresses, rather, the aftermath of the destructive act—the reverting of these urban places to their pre-urbanized state. In this sense, Chapter 2 is a sequel to Chapter 1 in which the creation of the world is undone. But in a more specific sense, I find that in a manner tailored to his needs, Zephaniah is calling upon the perception of the world that informs Genesis 10. The "we" and "they" of this chapter are Shem and Ham. When "we, the shepherds" will triumph over "them, the city-dwellers," their cities will fall and their land will become pastures for sheep. Zephaniah has taken the geopolitical situation of the late seventh century B.C.E. and couched it in the traditional enmity of Shem for Ham—i.e., Israel for the Canaanites. Judah's immediate neighbors can easily be seen as "Canaanites." Assyria, too far removed to be part of Canaan and never in the realm of possessable land, is Canaan's brother, Cush.

Why is Egypt omitted? Egypt was a great world power, Judah's neighbor, and also a son of Ham, so its omission deserves comment. If the prophecy is directed specifically against Assyria and its loyal vassals, there is no reason to mention Egypt as long as Egypt was not yet allied with Assyria (see Haak, "Zephaniah's Oracles Against the Nations"). Or, as H. Cazelles suggested, Zephaniah may have belonged to a pro-Egyptian party (such a party existed at various times in the late monarchy). Zephaniah did not have to include every nation; just those that fit his purpose.

Where is Japheth in this picture? To be sure, the nations of Japheth were not of major political importance at this time, and so they are largely omitted from this scenario. But there is a hint of Japheth in v. 11, in "the islands of the nations" (which occurs only here and in Gen 10:5).

The islands of the nations are the descendants of the sons of Japheth. Among the sons of Japheth in Gen 10:2 are Gomer, identified with the Cimmerians, and Madai, the Medes; and one of the sons of Gomer is Ashkenaz, identified with the Scythians. Perhaps Zephaniah is making a veiled reference to these groups, and others like them, who figure in Assyrian history, sometimes as friends and sometimes as foes, beginning in the time of Esarhaddon. It is not clear if the Scythians actually penetrated as far as Judah, but they certainly wrought havoc in parts of the Assyrian empire (see Oded, "Judah and the Exile," 467). According to our v. 11, the islands of the nations will acknowledge and worship the Lord. They will not be destroyed like Philistia, the transjordanian nations, and Assyria, probably because they are not perceived as enemies. They are simply "the distant islands which have not heard my name and not seen my glory" (Isa 66:19); but now they will come to know the power of God.

Zephaniah's prophecy against the nations, like other prophecies of this type, portrays a world in which Judah's enemies will disappear (cf. Chapter 3). The message becomes more compelling because political reality is set within the framework of an accepted myth. The contemporary political situation is made to look like a realization of the tradition of Gen 9:26–28: Canaan will become subservient to his brothers, and Japheth will reside in the tents of Shem.

VI. Prophecy Against the Overbearing City (3:1–13)

◆

3 ¹Woe, sullied and polluted, the overbearing city.
²She does not obey, she does not accept discipline.
In the Lord she does not trust, to her God she does not draw
near.
³Her officials within her are roaring lions,
Her judges are wolves of the evening,
Who do not gnaw till the morning.
⁴Her prophets are audacious, people of treachery,
Her priests profane the holy, corrupt the teaching.
⁵The Lord is righteous in her midst,
He does no wrong.
Morning after morning he displays his judgment in the light
which never fails,
But the wrongdoer ignores condemnation.
⁶I cut off nations, their corner towers were left desolate,
I turned their streets into ruins, empty of passersby.
Their cities were laid waste, empty of people, without
inhabitants.
⁷I thought: Surely you will fear me, you will accept discipline.
And her dwelling will not be cut off, in accord with all that I
have ordained against her.
But in fact they promptly corrupted all their deeds.
⁸Therefore wait for me, says the Lord,
[Wait] for the day when I rise once and for all.

For my verdict is to gather nations, to assemble kingdoms,
To pour upon them my anger, the full fierceness of my wrath,
For by the fire of my passion the entire earth will be consumed.
⁹After that I will turn over to peoples pure speech,
So all of them will invoke the name of the Lord,
And worship him with one accord.
¹⁰From beyond the rivers of Cush
Atarai Fair Puzai will bring my offering.
¹¹On that day you shall not be condemned for all your deeds
     whereby you have rebelled against me.
For then I will remove from your midst those elated with
     pridefulness.
And you will no longer continue to be haughty on my holy
     mount.
¹²And I will leave in your midst poor and humble folk,
And they shall take refuge in the name of the Lord.
¹³The remnant of Israel will do no wrong and will speak no lies;
No deceitful tongue will be found in their mouths.
Truly they will graze and lie down with none to disturb them.

NOTES

3:1. This *hoy* oracle is the counterpart to the *hoy* oracle which begins at 2:5. The doomed city is not named, but the description of its offenses makes clear that it is Jerusalem. A few interpreters, including the Peshitta, understand it to refer to Nineveh since it follows the oracle against that city; but Nineveh would not be criticized for the failures of its judges, priests, and prophets.

Sullied. Commentators are fairly evenly divided on the root of *mwrʾh*. Some take it from *rʾy*, "excrement, filth." (Medieval Jewish commentators point to Nah 3:6 and Lev 1:16.) This meaning parallels the following word, "polluted." Others derive it from *mrh*, "to rebel," explaining that final *he* verbs sometimes imitate the forms of final *ʾalep* verbs. This sense parallels v. 2: "she does not obey." A third possibility, less often found, is *yrʾ*, "frightful, awesome." (Ibn Ezra offers all three options.) Sabottka and O'Connor take it from *mrʾh*, "to be fat."

126

Polluted. From *gʾl* II, "polluted"—cf. Isa 59:3; Mal 1:7. The city is polluted from its idolatrous or syncretistic worship. The ancient Versions take the root as *gʾl* I, "to redeem." Malbim, rather idiosyncratically, interprets the description to mean that Jerusalem was feared or revered (*yrʾ*) by the other nations in the times of Hezekiah and Josiah (because of their reforms), and that it would be redeemed (*gʾl* I) from the hand of Assyria.

Overbearing. From the root *ynh*, "to oppress." Cf. Exod 22:20; Jer 25:38. LXX and Vulgate have "dove" for *ywnh*; Peshitta has "Jonah," thus taking the city as Nineveh. Some would emend to *zona*, "harlot"— cf. Isa 1:21.

The Hebrew employs the definite article—lit. "the overbearing city"—as it does in 2:1. The article may, as in 2:1, indicate the vocative, and so could be translated "Woe, you overbearing city." The fact that it is followed only by third-person references (unlike *hoy* in 2:5) does not rule out the possibility of the vocative, for third-person forms often follow a vocative *hoy* oracle (see Hillers, "*Hoy* and *Hoy*-Oracles"). Nevertheless, I have opted for a literal translation, which implies a third person. Cf. Isa 31:1–3 for a similar construction. Actually, too much is made of the difference between second- and third-person usage in these oracles. They are, in essence, addresses to fictive audiences—a fictive vocative, as it were—that is the opposite of addressing someone who is present in the third person. Both of these types of discourse blur the distinction between second and third person.

2. Roberts correctly notes that the clauses with finite verbs following *hoy* should be construed as unmarked relative clauses, and he translates "who did not listen . . . who did not accept . . ." But he reverts to independent clauses in the second half of the verse. For the sake of English style, which does not favor a chain of relative clauses, I have translated all of these clauses uniformly as independent clauses.

I have rendered the perfective verbs in the present tense. Translators are inconsistent here. My sense is that these perfectives signify a habitual state or recurrent condition (see Waltke and O'Connor, 485).

Accept discipline. An oft-found expression in Jeremiah and Proverbs. The Targum interprets this verse as referring to the rejection of the chastisement of the prophets.

3. There are two difficult phrases in this verse which have elicited a large number of conjectures from earliest times until the present. What is clear is that the officials and judges are compared to lions and wolves, ferocious wild animals preying on the weak.

Roaring lions. Lion imagery is common in the prophets; the animal is noted for its roar and its ferocity (Brensinger, 76–77). According to Isa 5:29; Ezek 22:25; and Amos 3:4, the lion roars when it is about to seize its prey. Perhaps the image is of officials pouncing on their victims.

Wolves of the evening. This is a crux, both here and in Hab 1:8. Cf. Jer 5:6, "wolf of the steppes/desert." Zalcman, *ET* 91, has summarized the possible interpretations:

(1) "wolves of the evening"—so Targum, Peshitta, Vulgate, and some modern translations. Compare perhaps Gen 49:27. Ball, 217, observes that vv. 3–4 and Genesis 49 share eight words: *ʾrywt, zʾby, ʿrb, grmw, lbqr, pḥzym, ḥllw, ḥmsw.* Genesis 49 is largely a criticism of the tribal leaders or ancestors, and Zephaniah is criticizing the current leadership.

(2) "wolves of Arabia"—so LXX. Roberts, 92, notes that this rendering presupposes the MT but indicates the translators' dissatisfaction with "wolves of the evening."

(3) "wolves of the steppe/desert"—so some modern translations. This is based on the equation of *ʿrb* with *ʿrbwt* of Jer 5:6. Cf. also Isa 21:13.

(4) "hungry wolves"—so Good News Bible. This takes *ʿrb* as a metathesis for *rʿb.* This is perhaps hinted at by Ibn Ezra.

Zalcman cleverly translates "ravening wolves," thereby capturing the soundplay and wordplay. He also suggests a sly allusion to Oreb and Zeeb, princes of Midian in Jud 7:25; 8:3—cf. Ps 83:12.

Ben Zvi adds to the possibilities by suggesting that *ʿrb* be linked to the term in Exod 12:38 and Neh 13:3, "mixed multitude." He sees a double entendre, employing both the contrast between "morning" and "evening" and the "pack character" of wolves. Ben Zvi also notes that despite the lack of verbal identity, this metaphor resembles the one in Ezek 22:27.

Malbim sees a contrast between the lions (officials) who prey publicly on the people and the wolves of the evening (judges) who do so secretly, at night, by taking bribes.

Who do not gnaw till the morning. The presence of "morning" gives support to "evening" in the preceding phrase. The verb *grmw* is generally understood as "gnaw a bone" (cf. Num 24:8; Ezek 23:34), and from the context the sense may be that they do not leave a bone by morning. This would make the judges more voracious than wolves, who do not eat the bones of their prey. O'Connor understands the particle *lʾ* as an emphatic, not as a negative, hence "they gnaw at morning."

Ben Zvi prefers the extended meaning "to have strength" (by analogy with *ʿṣm* and the usage of *grm*, "crush," in Num 24:8), yielding the idea that the wolves attack at night in packs and have no strength left by morning.

The word *grm* has also been taken, by metathesis, as *gmr*, "finish," yielding a similar sense: "They do not finish [eating] until morning." Stenzel, *VT* 1, emended to *gwrym*, "lions," yielding "her judges are wolves in the evening and lions in the morning." The numerous attempts to explain or emend demonstrate that this is a crux.

4. *Audacious.* The root *pḥz* has the sense of "reckless, unstable." The prophets brazenly utter words that God has not given them. Cf. Jer 23:32.

People of treachery. By their false prophecies, the prophets deceive and mislead the people. Hebrew *bgdwt* is an abstract noun serving as the *nomen rectum* in the construct chain *ʾnšy bgdwt*. Malbim construed it as the feminine plural participle, interpreting "husbands of traitorous wives."

Profane the holy. In contradiction to Lev 22:15. The donations and offerings brought for cultic purposes were to be eaten only by the priests and authorized members of their families. The meaning seems to have broadened to include any lack of distinction between the holy and the profane, as in Ezek 22:26. Leviticus and Ezekiel employ the plural, "holy things," while here we have the singular *qodeš*, "holy thing."

Corrupt the teaching. NJPS aptly renders "they give perverse rulings." The *tora* was the domain of the priests—cf. Jer 18:18; Ezek 7:26; Mic 3:11; and de Vaux, *Ancient Israel*, 353–55. It was their duty to decide cultic questions and even civil and criminal cases (Deut 17:8–13). DNF would stress that the offense involves lawless behavior on the part of the priests.

The order of these two clauses is reversed in Ezek 22:26, and from the construction there it seems likely that they indicate two aspects of one transgression, not two separate transgressions: the intentionally wrong interpretation of *tora* which permitted the profaning of the holy.

5. *Morning after morning.* Hebrew *bbqr bbqr* picks up the wordplay with "evening" and "morning" in v. 3 and the soundplay with *bqrbh*, "in her midst," in vv. 3 and 5. For another occurrence of this expression see Exod 16:21.

He displays his judgment in the light. God's judgment is manifest in the dawning of each day. The morning light is a sign of God's judgment, and just as the light dawns each day, so will God's judgment always be present. The connection between judgment and (sun)light is similar to Psalm 19 and reflects this broader ancient near eastern concept (e.g., Shamash is the god of the sun and the god of justice). Ps 37:6 takes this idea and makes it a simile: "He will cause your righteousness to shine forth like the light." (This has provoked some to emend *l>wr* to *k>wr* in our verse.) But Zeph 3:5 is not a simile; it does not mean that God's judgment is *like* the light, but rather that God makes his judgment visible in the light (= sun). The construction *ntn* X *l-* means "to make/ turn X into Y" (cf. Jer 9:10); so literally our phrase would mean "He makes his judgment into the light."

I have taken the entire phrase as one thought, as do MT, LXX, Vulgate, and KJV. Modern translations and commentaries tend to split it into two parallel stichs. NRSV is representative: "Every morning he renders his judgment, each dawn without fail." Hebrew *l>wr* then becomes an adverb parallel to *bbqr bbqr* instead of the object of the verb. (Roberts takes *l>wr* as "twilight," thereby creating a merismus with "morning.") This is a possible interpretation, but less meaningful than the one I have proposed.

But the wrongdoer ignores condemnation. The conjunction is best understood as adversative, contrasting God's expectation with the mentality of the wicked. The subject of this clause shifts abruptly from God to the wrongdoer, the verbal form shifts from an imperfect to a participle, and the wording is laconic—giving the impression to some that the clause does not fit naturally. (NEB omits it.) Commentaries and translations have wrestled with the phrase in a number of ways, most rendering "But the wrongdoer knows no shame." This, in my opinion, does not capture the correct nuance. NJPS construes the clause with the following verse, as the reason for the punishment. Ball renders "He does not know the unjust men of shame," taking "the Lord" as the subject of the clause. Ben Zvi discusses but rejects this possibility. The suggestion (Ball, Sabottka) that *bšt* stands for Baal is not helpful.

My own understanding is based on the broader meanings of *ydᶜ* and *bšt*, and on the syntax. The same syntax, (*l*) *ydᶜ* + subject + object, is found in Ps 37:18; Prov 12:10; 29:7; Job 28:13. The range of meanings of *l ydᶜ* includes "not know, not discern, not recognize, not heed, ignore." For "not heed, ignore" see Isa 42:25. The noun *bšt*, which occurs also in 3:19, and the verb *bwš*, in 3:11, are not limited to English "to be ashamed," but include also "reproach, disgrace, condemn, discomfit, confound." The sense is not that the subject of this verb will feel shame, but that he or she will be disgraced, condemned, or confounded. Hence the meaning of our phrase is that the wrongdoer ignores the condemnation, guilt, and ruination that his wrongdoing brings. For *bšt* used in parallelism with "sin, guilt" see Hab 2:20. In the context of this verse, the meaning is that while God's justice is ever-present, and according to this justice the wrongdoer is condemned, the wrongdoer nevertheless ignores the condemnation and continues to do wrong.

6. *Nations.* NEB renders "proud," reading *gᵓym* for *gwym*.

Corner towers. Cf. 1:16.

Empty of . . . Cf. 2:5. The disappearance of the population is stressed through threefold repetition.

Were laid waste. Compare Jer 2:15; 4:7; 9:11, where the verb is *nṣh*. Here the root is *ṣdh* II, unknown elsewhere in the Bible but cognate to Aramaic *ṣdy* (Ben Zvi).

7. This verse, too, shifts grammatical person—from a reference to Jerusalem in the second person, in the quoted thought of God, to the third person, as God, still speaking in the first person, resumes his discourse about Jerusalem. The Lord thought that his destruction of other nations, being an example of God's mighty punishment, would lead Jerusalem to fear him, and so avert its own destruction. But the people of Jerusalem continued eagerly in their corrupt ways.

Surely. On the emphatic use of *ᵓak* see Muraoka, 129–30.

Fear. The fear of the Lord and the acceptance of discipline *(mwsr)* are the basic tenets of wisdom literature—cf. Prov 1:7; 9:10.

Her dwelling. MT *mᶜwnh.* Jerusalem is personified as having a dwelling. But Jerusalem represents the people, and thus in a literal sense the dwelling is Jerusalem. The meaning is that the people will lose their city.

LXX reads "from her eyes"—*mᶜynyh* for *mᶜwnh.* Accepting this reading, Roberts translates "And there will not be cut off from her eyes all the punishment that I brought upon her." But this goes against the apparent intent of the verse, which is to avert the punishment. Roberts explains by interpreting the previous verse as referring to punishment that has already come to Jerusalem, not punishment of other nations. This previous punishment was presumably to serve as a warning or teach a lesson regarding the future punishment. NJPS, also accepting "from her eyes," treats the verse differently: "And the punishment I brought on them [Heb. her] would not be lost on her [lit. cut off from her vision]." NJPS takes v. 6 to refer to other nations, but must construe the pronominal suffix "her" in the phrase *pqdty ᶜlyh* as referring to a different "her" from "her eyes." That is, "her [= Jerusalem's] eyes" but "I assigned against her [= other nations]." The expression "cut off from the eyes" is not otherwise attested; it may be modeled on "cut off from the mouth" (Jer 7:28; Joel 1:5). Despite the long tradition of reading "from her eyes," this reading does not make better sense than the MT, but only brings problems of its own.

A third possibility exists, although I have not seen it proposed anywhere. That is to read *meᶜawwonah,* "from her guilt/punishment." The sense would be: "But nothing at all will be cut off from her punishment that I ordained against her. For indeed, they promptly corrupted all their deeds."

In accord with all that I have ordained against her. One must assume an unexpressed *k-* before *kl.* Cf. Bolle. *Pqd ᶜl* is generally taken in a negative sense, "to visit punishment on." NEB's "in the hope that she would remember all my instructions" and REB's "all the commands I laid on her" take *pqd ᶜl* in a positive sense. These translations must rearrange the order of the clauses to make this meaning intelligible.

But in fact. Hebrew *ʾkn,* an asseverative-emphatic particle which

132

sometimes "indicates a turning-point in thought of the speaker and expresses the reality in opposition to his previous doubt or false presupposition" (Muraoka, 132). For this sense see Isa 49:4; 53:4; Jer 3:20; Ps 82:7.

Promptly. Hebrew *hškymw,* a verbal form functioning adverbially, meaning literally "to rise early," that is, "to do eagerly."

8. The addressee is unclear; perhaps the same as in v. 7, that is, Jerusalem. If so, Jerusalem, not yet convinced of God's power (in vv. 6–7), will be convinced when he again rises to destroy the nations.

Once and for all. Interpreting the Hebrew *le'ad* as *la'ad,* "forever" (so the Vulgate). Most modern translations follow the LXX, reading *le'ed,* "as a witness." The MT as it is vocalized means "for booty"—cf. Gen 49:17; Isa 33:23; Bolle, and Ball ("for the prey"). Sabottka suggests "from the throne," following a suggestion of Dahood. Ehrlich emends to *l'rk,* "to array in battle."

The imagery of wrath and fire echoes 1:15 and 2:2, and the same phraseology, "the entire earth will be consumed by the fire of his/my passion" occurs here and in 1:18.

9. *After that.* Literally, "for then." The idea is that after the conflagration, all will acknowledge the Lord (see Bolle).

Turn over. Literally, "change," i.e., God will change the impure speech, whereby the peoples invoke other gods, into pure speech, whereby they will invoke only the Lord. Cf. 1 Sam 10:9 for a similar usage of "change."

To peoples. The Murabba'at text reads *'l h'mym,* "on the peoples" (*'l,* "on," and *'l,* "to," may alternate). The MT's reading may be an instance of the omission of the definite article in poetry, with the sense of "the peoples" (DNF). Some scholars would prefer *'my,* "my people," but the idea seems to be universal worship of the Lord, reminiscent of, or actually going beyond, the idea in 2:11.

Pure speech. Ps 15:2–3 and 24:4 suggest that proper speech is a requirement for entrance into the cult. Here the idea seems to be that the impure speech of idolatry is replaced with pure speech by means of which one can praise the Lord. Or perhaps we should understand "pure speech" as the opposite of "unintelligible speech" which prevents communication between the parties (Isa 33:19; Ezek 3:5, 6).

With one accord. The idiom *škm ʾḥd*, literally "with one shoulder," is unattested elsewhere but its meaning is clear from the context.

10. *Rivers of Cush.* This verse most closely resembles Isa 18:1 and 7, with its mention of "beyond the rivers of Cush" and the idea of bringing gifts to God from people in a remote place. In Isa 18:1 and Zeph 3:10, as in 2:12, most scholars understand "Cush" as Ethiopia, and the "rivers of Cush" as the Blue Nile and the White Nile. However, when "Cush" clearly signifies "Ethiopia" it occurs in the company of other lands, like Egypt or Put, or in geographical contexts like "from India to Cush." The one exception, "topaz of Cush" (Job 28:19), is paralleled a few verses earlier by "the gold of Ophir." But in our verse there is no reason to single out "Ethiopia." In light of my interpretation of "Cush" in 2:12, I would see here, too, a reference to the Mesopotamian Cush (Ibn Ezra glosses "the rivers of Cush" in Isa 18:1 with "the kingdom of Assyria"). More specifically, it refers to the rivers of the Garden of Eden, one of which was the "Gihon which wanders through the whole land of Cush" (Gen 2:13). E. A. Speiser interpreted "Cush" in Gen 2:13 as a Mesopotamian location (derived from "Kassites"), related to the Cush of Gen 10:7–8 (see "The Rivers of Paradise"). Ball, 244–52, makes a strong case for the Mesopotamian rivers-of-Paradise motif in Isa 18:1 and Zeph 3:10 (although he does not see Cush as Mesopotamian in 2:12). He points out that the Garden-of-God motif is often associated with the Zion tradition, as may be the case in v. 11. I do not wish to argue for an intensely mythological allusion here, but for an allusion that would convey the remoteness of the location. The point is not whether these rivers are in Mesopotamia or in Africa, but that the main thrust of the phrase is to evoke a far-off place, at the ends of the earth, from which people will bring offerings to the Lord. For that, a reference to Eden seems more apt than a reference to Ethiopia, for Ethiopia is part of the known world—far, to be sure, but not impossibly far—while the rivers of Eden are at the ends of the earth, the farthest place imaginable. Similarly Utnapishtim (Epic of Gilgamesh XI) dwells "far off, at the mouth of the rivers."

The crux of this verse is *ʿtry bt pwṣy*, omitted in some LXX manuscripts and the Peshitta, rendered strangely in the other Versions, and deemed unintelligible by many. I see no possibility of solving the problem. I offer some of the most common suggestions here; for others see Ball, 175–76, and Ben Zvi.

Atarai. Hebrew ʿtry, usually understood as "my supplicants," from the root ʿtr, "to entreat" (Gen 25:21). Segal suggests also "odor of incense" (Ezek 8:11). Most medieval Jewish commentaries consider this and the following term the names of foreign peoples or lands.

Fair Puzai. Hebrew bt pwṣy is taken as a geographical name by NJPS, which also mentions an emendation to "Zion." It is more commonly rendered "daughter of my dispersed," a qal passive participle of pwṣ. Roberts mentions the correction to btpwṣh, "in the dispersion." Smith, ICC, emends to Put, a country mentioned along with Cush in, for example, Gen 10:6; Ezek 38:5.

The vocabulary and syntax permit several interpretations:

(1) "My supplicants, Fair Puzai (= distant nations) will bring my offering." This is the most common interpretation.

(2) "My supplicants, Fair dispersed (= Israel) will bring my offering."

(3) "My supplicants, Fair dispersed (= Israel) they (= other nations) will bring as my offering." This is more metaphorical, reflecting Isa 66:20, according to which the other nations will bring Israel out of dispersion to Jerusalem (cf. Ben Zvi).

Much of the discussion centers on whether this is a reference to Judean exiles in Egypt or Nubia who will return, as a rendering "daughter of my dispersed" would suggest. If so, it must refer to a period after Josiah, probably the period immediately preceding and/or following the destruction of Jerusalem. It would thus be a later addition (if the rest of the book was written in the time of Josiah) or an indication of the lateness of the book. More likely, however, the reference is not to Judean exiles but to foreign nations who will recognize the Lord. I see in vv. 9 and 10 the idea of universal worship of the God of Israel.

11. *On that day.* On the day when I rise—v. 8—which is the Day of the Lord.

Shall not be condemned. That is, your deeds will no longer lead to your punishment and disgrace before God and other nations. See the NOTE on 3:5. Most commentators understand this phrase to mean "you will not be ashamed of your deeds," but the issue is not whether Israel feels shame, but whether it is put to shame. God will remove Israel's guilt and shame by removing the cause of them—the prideful element of society. Ben Zvi notes that *bwš* ("condemned, confounded, shamed") and *ḥsh* ("take refuge"—v. 12) are a syntagmatic pair, occurring in Ps 25:20; 31:2; 71:1. The usage in these psalms makes it clear that *bwš* means "confounded" (NJPS has "disappointed"), not "feel ashamed."

Elated with pridefulness. Literally, "your exulters in pridefulness." This refers here to the opposite of the poor and humble folk, that is, the upper classes as opposed to the lower classes. Cf. 1:8–13. The same idiom occurs in Isa 13:3 in the prophecy against Babylon, where it has a rather different nuance. Ball, 177–78, 294, following the LXX and the Vulgate, renders "the exultations of your pride."

To be haughty. As Ben Zvi explains, this means to rely on yourselves instead of on God. It echoes 1:12, 18.

My holy mount. The Temple Mount or perhaps, by extension, Jerusalem as a whole.

12. *Poor and humble folk.* The lowly, those who are not elated with pridefulness. These are the ones who will be spared, for according to 2:3, they have performed God's command.

Take refuge in the name of the Lord. The more common phrase, found some thirty times in the Bible, is "take refuge in the Lord." Only here is it "take refuge in the name of the Lord." But the sense is the same: to take refuge in the person of the Lord, rather than in something else, like themselves or their wealth. Cf. Ps 118:8: "It is better to take refuge in the Lord than to trust in human beings." Again, this echoes 2:3, and also 3:2: "In the Lord she does not trust."

13. The LXX and several modern translations connect "the remnant of Israel" with v. 12, making it the subject of "shall take refuge."

The remnant of Israel. Previously we have "the remnant of the House of Judah" (2:7) and "the remnant of my people" (2:9). Following Ben Zvi (234), I would distinguish the concept of "the remnant of the House of Judah" from "the remnant of Israel." The former is a geographical or political concept, while the latter is, in Ben Zvi's words, a "religious, ideological concept." This usage is obvious in the expression "the Lord of Hosts, God of Israel" (2:9); one does not speak of "the God of Judah." As a religious or ideological concept, "Israel" refers to the people in its earliest days and also to the people as a whole even after the division of the monarchy. It is found in this sense in a number of prophetic books (along with its narrower, political designation for the Northern Kingdom). It continues to be used in exilic and postexilic sources, where only the people of Judah can be meant, to signify members of the religious community (e.g., Ezra 2:70). Jeremiah, Ezekiel, and Deutero-Isaiah also use it to refer to the Judean exiles. (For a fuller listing of the occurrences and their usages see *TDOT* VI, 397–420.) In our verse, and also in vv. 14–15, it bears a related meaning; it refers to the people of Jerusalem who will have survived the catastrophe that God will have brought upon the world and upon Judah. (See NOTE to v. 14.)

Do no wrong. Like the Lord, who does no wrong, and in contrast to those who do (3:5).

Deceitful tongue. This may echo the pure speech of 3:9, although there it refers to all the nations, who will invoke the name of the Lord, and here it refers to the remnant of Israel, who will speak truthfully. This particular phrase, *lšwn trmyt*, is found only here, but compare the related phrase, *lšwn rmyh*, in Mic 6:12; Ps 120:2, 3; Job 27:4. The Hebrew ʿwlh and *rmyh* (or *mrmh*) occur in conjunction in Ps 43:1; Job 13:7; 27:4. The word *lšwn*, usually feminine, is masculine here.

Truly. The particle *ky* has here an asseverative-emphatic use; see Muraoka, 158–64.

Graze and lie down with none to disturb them. "Graze and lie down" recalls 2:7, but the addition of "with none to disturb them" makes clear that this is a different image, one of peace and security. The metaphor of Israel as sheep is used elsewhere as a metaphor for the return from exile (cf. Jer 23:1–8; Ezekiel 34). Here it is less certain that a return is being described (unless one interprets v. 10 as referring to Israel). Rather, the pastoral metaphor indicates that the enemies of the remnant of Israel, both external and internal, are no longer present to endanger God's flock.

COMMENT

This *hoy* oracle is in some ways the counterpart of the *hoy* oracle in 2:5–15. It begins with the same word and ends with the image of shepherding, but with an important reversal. The negative image of urban areas reduced to pastureland or wasteland is gone. In its place is the positive image of pasturing in peace and security. So instead of ending on a note of destruction, it ends on a note of hope for the future. It also contrasts markedly the fate of Canaan and Assyria with the fate of Israel.

Verses 1–8 have affinities to Ezek 22:23–31: "uncleansed land . . . her band of prophets is in her midst like a roaring lion tearing prey . . . her priests have corrupted my teaching and profaned my holy things . . . her officials are in her midst like wolves tearing prey, to spill blood, to destroy life for the purpose of gaining profit . . . and her prophets daub the wall for them with plaster, prophesying falsely and divining for them deceitfully . . . I have poured upon them my anger, in the fire of my wrath I have made an end of them." These affinities are specific enough to suggest a more than coincidental relationship, but it is not clear whether Ezekiel borrowed from Zephaniah or whether both had recourse to a common tradition. (See Ben Zvi for further discussion. H. L. Ginsberg, *JBL* 69, suggested that Isa 5:14–17 once resembled Zeph 3:1–13 more closely than it does now and served as a model for Zephaniah. The Zephaniah passage, in turn, was employed by Ezekiel.)

The addressee of this oracle is not named explicitly, but from what follows it would seem to be Jerusalem. It is also difficult to understand all of the images and the relationship of various sections to one another. Nevertheless, a coherent message can be perceived. Jerusalem has taken on the characteristics of its leaders, polluted and arrogant. Yet despite the corruption of all areas of public life—by government officials, judges, prophets, and priests—God remains, untainted by injustice and corruption, in the city. His righteousness shines forth every day. Yet God's just condemnation is ignored by the evildoers. And the destructions that he had brought upon other nations have failed to serve as an admonition to Jerusalem's leadership. But, warns the Lord, in time they will also receive punishment, and then they will understand the error of their ways. For the proper recognition of the Lord is inevitable. All nations will come to acknowledge him. At that time, Jerusalem's sins will no longer be held against her, for those causing the sins, the haughty elite, will have been removed, and only the humble God-fearing folk will remain. This remnant will speak and behave correctly, and will dwell secure.

The emphasis on punishment and destruction, so vividly presented in Chapters 1 and 2, is here muted. Though verse 8 does contain a reference to God's wrath, and harks back to 1:18, the emphasis in this section is on the contrast between the present corruption and the future which will be free of corruption.

VII. JOY TO JERUSALEM
(3:14–20)

◆

¹⁴Sing, Fair Zion,
  Shout aloud, Israel,
  Be glad and exult with all your heart, Fair Jerusalem.
¹⁵The Lord has commuted your sentence,
  He has cleared away your foe.
  The King of Israel, the Lord, is in your midst,
  You will no longer fear evil.
¹⁶On that day it will be said to Jerusalem: Do not be afraid;
  To Zion: Do not be disheartened.
¹⁷The Lord your God is in your midst,
  A warrior who brings victory.
  He rejoices over you with gladness,
  He keeps silent in his love,
  He delights over you with song.
¹⁸Those grieving from the festival whom I have gathered were from
        you.
  A burden on her, a reproach.
¹⁹Behold, I will deal with all your tormentors at that time,
  And I will rescue the lame, and the strayed I will gather in.
  And I will turn their condemnation into praise and fame
        throughout the whole earth.
²⁰At that time I will bring you [home].
  And at the time that I gather you,

Indeed, I will make you famed and praised among all the
  peoples of the earth,
When I restore your fortunes before your eyes, said the Lord.

NOTES

14. *Sing.*   Happiness and rejoicing are expressed by raising the voice
in song and shouting. Cf. Isa 12:6; 54:1; Zech 2:14.

Israel.   The people of Jerusalem. "Israel" is parallel to "Fair Zion"
and "Fair Jerusalem." That is, the people of Jerusalem are called "Israel."
So, too, in v. 13 "the remnant of Israel" are those in Jerusalem. Compare
Lam 2:1 where "Fair Zion" is "the majesty of Israel." Cf. Ezek 12:19;
21:7. See also the NOTE on v. 13.

15. The judgment or verdict *(mšpṭ)* mentioned in v. 8 is here set
aside. The verdict had been destruction. Now God commutes the
sentence and turns back the enemy. On the relationship of these two
ideas see Ben Zvi, 243.

Commuted your sentence.   Or: "dropped the charges against you."
Mišpaṭayik is in the plural. Usually the plural signifies "decrees, statutes," and is often found in conjunction with *ḥqym*; the term for
"sentence, verdict, punishment" is normally in the singular, *mšpṭ*. The
exception is Jeremiah, where the plural is found—Jer 4:12; 12:1; 39:5 =
52:9. Notice that the parallel to the last reference in 2 Kgs 25:6 has the
singular. (The meaning is "to pronounce the verdict," not "bring to
trial.") Cf. also Ezek 5:8, where there seems to be a play on words with
"statutes." Thus there is no problem with the usage of this form. But
following the Targum's "false judges," Smith and others revocalize to
mešopṭayik, "your judges" (cf. Job 9:15), which then is seen as parallel to
"your foe."

Cleared away.   Hebrew *pnh* in the *piʿel* occurs in the Latter Prophets
always in the sense of "clear the way [*drk*]"—Isa 40:3; 57:14; 62:10; Mal
3:1. In Gen 24:31 and Lev 14:36 it is used with *byt* to mean "clear/make
ready the house." In Ps 80:10 it lacks a direct object. NJPS translates
"cleared a place," while Bolle interprets the verse to mean "cleared out
the nations" (cf. v. 9). This is the closest to our verse in Zephaniah.

Your foe.   The MT has a singular, though many prefer to read "foes" in the plural, as do some Masoretic mss., the Murabba'at text, and the LXX, Targum, and Peshitta. Many think that the plural makes better sense; but, alternatively, one may construe the singular as a collective (Ball, Bolle, Ben Zvi), or, more precisely, as a "class noun" (Waltke and O'Connor, 114–15), in which a singular indicates a particular class, e.g., "the lion is the king of the beasts." Compare *rᶜh ṣᵓn* = "shepherds" in Gen 47:3; *hsbl* = "burden-bearers" in Neh 4:4. "Enemy" (definite or indefinite) often occurs in this last sense, especially in Psalms.

The enemy may be the one through whom judgment would have been achieved, that is, foreign nations; or the enemy within, on account of whom the judgment was issued—the prideful ones of v. 11. Attempts to identify one particular enemy, real or ideological (e.g., Assyria, Baal, or an arch-enemy of God), are unnecessary and forced.

King of Israel, the Lord. For the Lord as King of Israel see Isa 44:6 (cf. 41:21). The implication is that when the Lord is recognized as king, pridefulness and disobedience are gone and God's protection is present.

In your midst. *Bqrb* occurs in Chapter 3 in vv. 3, 5, 11, 12, 15, 17, emphasizing that sinners were in Jerusalem's midst, and that, conversely, God was or would be in her midst.

Fear evil. The form of the verb in the MT indicates that its root is *yrᵓ*, "to fear." This is supported by the note to Isa 60:5 in the Masorah Parva (Ben Zvi), and by the presence of the idiom in Ps 23:4. The Vulgate and Targum render "fear evil." Most modern commentaries do likewise. However, *yrᵓ* and *rᵓh* are easily confused. Ben Zvi notes that the "Second Rabbinic Bible (Ben Hayyim)" reads *trᵓy*, suggesting the root *rᵓh*. The expression *rᵓh rᶜ*, "to see (experience) evil," occurs in Hab 1:13. The LXX and the Peshitta, as well as Abravanel and KJV, interpret it this way. Note that the verb *yrᵓ* occurs in v. 16 also. Notice the soundplay on the roots *rᶜh*, "graze" (v. 13), *rwᶜ*, "shout" (v. 14), *yrᵓ* or *rᵓh* and *rᶜᶜ* (v. 15), *yrᵓ* (v. 16).

16. *On that day.* In the future, after Jerusalem's sentence has been commuted. There will then be no cause to fear God's punishment.

It will be said. The passive impersonal form emphasizes the recipient of the message while it suppresses the speaker.

Do not be afraid. This expression is common in prophecies of encouragement (e.g., Isa 41:14; 44:2). On *yrʾ* in the sense of "anxious" see Gruber, *VT* 40.

Do not be disheartened. Literally, "Let not your hands weaken." This expression is less common but occurs in 2 Sam 4:1; Isa 13:7; Jer 6:24; 50:43; Ezek 7:17; 21:12; Ezra 4:4; Neh 6:9; 2 Chr 15:7. It means "to be afraid, discouraged, in despair, unable to act." It is often associated with a verb of fear, *yrʾ* or *bhl*, or with other physiological descriptions of fear like the heart melting, the knees turning to water, or the spirit becoming faint. Its opposite is "be strong, take courage."

I have followed the MT's accents in subdividing the verse. This division preserves the parallelism between Jerusalem and Zion (which is also present in v. 14). However, it requires that the preposition *l* be understood before "Zion" (so KJV, Bolle). It is rare, but not unknown, for a preposition to be omitted before a noun in a series that it governs. Cf. Isa 48:14: "He will carry out his purpose against Babylonia; and his arm [against] Chaldeans." See Waltke and O'Connor, 222–23, and O'Connor, *HVS*, 310–11, for a discussion and other examples.

O'Connor (*HVS*, 261) accepts the MT's division but interprets the *l* as an emphatic, used as a vocative marker. He translates:

On that day it will be said:
Don't be afraid, Jerusalem.
Don't drop your hands, Zion.

Ball also interprets this way, as does Gruber, *VT* 40, 417–18. On the face of it, this sounds like better poetry, and *l* as a vocative marker is amply documented. However, in every other occurrence of *yeʾamer l-* the sense is always "it will be said to/about" (e.g., Isa 32:5; 61:6; 62:4; Jer 4:11; Ezek 13:12; Hos 2:1; Ps 87:5). Since this construction never introduces a vocative, I am reluctant to see one here.

Most recent translations and commentaries divide the verse as follows:

On that day it will be said to Jerusalem:
Do not fear, Zion,
Do not let your hands droop.

This does not require supplying a preposition but it strikes me as conforming less to the poetic style of the Bible.

17. There are echoes of v. 15, "the Lord is in your midst," and of v. 14, "gladness and song." In v. 14 Jerusalem was the one rejoicing; here God rejoices over Jerusalem. For this idea see also Isa 65:19; 62:5; Deut 30:9. Jerusalem is the joy of the whole earth—Isa 65:18; Ps 48:3; Lam 2:15.

A warrior who brings victory. Literally, a warrior who saves. God will save Jerusalem. It is not clear whether we should see this as a military image (especially if Jerusalem's enemy is within her), as an epithet for God, or simply as metaphoric language for a hero. See Jer 14:9 for a verse with several of the same phrases: "Why are you like a man who is stunned, / like a warrior who cannot bring victory? / Yet you are in our midst, Lord . . ." For *śwś/śyś*, "rejoice," in association with *gbwr* see Ps 19:6. The identification of God as a *gbwr* here may support those who view the same word in 1:14 as a reference to God.

He keeps silent in his love. The phrase is difficult, if not totally unintelligible. Moreover, it interrupts a perfectly comprehensible parallelism, creating the impression that this may not have been its original location. For that reason, some Ancient Versions and modern translations transpose it to the end of the verse and connect it with the following verse. It was understood by the LXX and the Peshitta as "he will renew you in his love"—reading *yeḥaddešek* for *yḥryš*. The Hebrew root *ḥrš* is usually taken from the word "to be silent," which Roberts extends to mean "he will soothe you." Other homophonous roots mean "to plough, engrave, plot"; but it is hard to see how they would make sense (despite a number of creative exegetical attempts). Ben Zvi opts for "he will be silent in his love," meaning that God will refrain from accusing Jerusalem of wrongdoing. This silence stands in contrast to God's singing which follows. This suggestion requires the least amount of juggling—it fits the grammar and the broader context, but still does not wholly explain this crux. Others emend to *yrḥš*, "he will stir up his love."

18. This verse is unintelligible. I have translated it as literally as possible, following the masoretic accents, in an attempt to reconstruct how the Masoretes may have understood it. It seems to mean that God has removed those in Jerusalem who were a reproach to her. Alterna-

tively, one might render "Those grieving from the festival whom I have gathered from you, were a burden on her, a reproach." (Cf. O'Connor for the last part of the verse.)

The Ancient Versions each render it differently and not completely coherently (see Ball, 187, for the renderings), suggesting difficulties long before the MT, which each Version sought to make sense of to the best of its ability. Modern translations continue the proliferation of renderings; Ball (188) found that of the more than thirty that he checked, no two were identical. We can do no more than offer a sampling of translations and possible interpretations of the individual words.

NJPS: He will soothe with His love [from v. 17]
      Those long disconsolate.
      I will take away from you the woe
      Over which you endured mockery.

NRSV: As on a day of festival [continuing from v. 17].
      I will remove disaster from you,
      so that you will not bear reproach for it.

KJV: I will gather them that are sorrowful for the solemn assembly,
      who are of thee, to whom the reproach of it was a burden.

Roberts: Those grieving far from the festival.
      I will gather up from you the 'Hey you!'
      So that one will not raise a reproach over you.

Ben Zvi: Those who are afflicted because they are deprived of festivals,
      I [YHWH] have gathered, they were from you,
      [they were] a sign on her, [they were] a [source of] mockery.

nwgy. A *nip'al* participle of *ygh*, in the construct state, meaning "those who are grieved, afflicted of" (cf. Lam 1:4).

mmw'd. "From [perhaps in a separative sense] the festival, fixed time." Ben Zvi suggests "those who are afflicted because they are deprived of the festivals." Roberts, following the LXX, connects this phrase with the difficult phrase in the previous verse, yielding "He will soothe in his love those grieving far from the festival."

'spty. "I (have) gathered."

mmk. "From you." But this preposition is unusual after "gathered."

hyw. "They were." But what is the subject? Perhaps this is to be linked with the preceding word—"they were from you." But the syntax is still elusive.

mś>t. "Burden" or, according to Ben Zvi, "signal" (Jer 6:1).

<lyh. "On her," referring to Jerusalem. Some emend to "on you," following the Peshitta and Targum, to match "from you."

ḥrph. "A reproach, shame, mockery" (cf. 2:8, 10).

19. *Deal with.* Hebrew *<śh* can bear this meaning—cf. Ezek 22:14; 23:25, and elsewhere. Alternatively, some have understood an implied word *klh*—"I will make an end to"—Vulgate, Targum, Ibn Ezra.

Rescue the lame . . . This phrase resembles Mic 4:6: "I will collect the lame and gather in the strayed." The Hebrew *ṣl<h* is a feminine signifying a collective. The image is of a shepherd rescuing his sheep from predators and keeping them from straying. The shepherd image is commonly used for kings in the ancient near east, and this metaphor continues the picture of God as king in v. 15. Although the reference could be to the downtrodden outcasts of Jerusalem, the language of vv. 19–20 sounds as if the reference is to the restoration of exiles from distant lands.

There is a slight syntactic irregularity at the end of the verse which has been dealt with in two ways:

1. Take the *m* at the end of *wśmtym* as enclitic; and take *bštm* as the object of the verb. I have chosen this option, as have Sabottka, O'Connor, NRSV, NJPS. Cf. v. 11—Jerusalem will no longer be condemned; her condemnation will be turned to praise.

2. "I will turn them into a praise and fame (i.e., praised and famed) in all the lands of their condemnation." This requires dropping the definite article from *h>rṣ*. This makes v. 19 similar to v. 20. The Vulgate and the Targum support this rendering, and many older and modern commentators, including Roberts and Ben Zvi, prefer it.

Ball renders "I will transform them into a praise, / And their shame into a name in all the earth."

20. The repetition of similar phrases in this verse, again with a slight syntactic irregularity, might suggest the possibility of dittography either in v. 19 or 20. But working against this is the reversal in the order of "praise" and "fame." Verse 20 supplies the reason that Israel will be lauded—the

return of its good fortunes. NJPS rearranges the clauses to make the sequence more logical, translating "At that time I will gather you, / And at [that] time I will bring you [home]." Cf. also NEB and REB. This verse echoes Jer 33:7–9.

I will bring. LXX reads "I will do good" (*ʾtyb*) for "I will bring" (*ʾbyʾ*).

Restore your fortunes. The plural is unusual; some mss. have the singular. The phrase also occurs in 2:7. The term may be interpreted as a return from captivity, or, more generally, as a restoration of Israel's fortunate position—cf. Job 42:10.

Your eyes. Some prefer to read "their eyes" instead of "your eyes" (NJPS, Roberts), meaning that the other nations will see the restoration of Israel's fortunes.

Ben Zvi points out that the book ends much the same way that Amos ends, pointing to an ideal future, including the phrase "restore the fortunes/captivity." However, Amos' vision is much more concrete and detailed, clearly stressing the return and the rebuilding. Zephaniah's prophecy is vaguer, offering no agricultural or urban scene.

COMMENT

The theme of this section is joyful song and praise. Jerusalem shall sing, for her sentence has been commuted and her enemies removed. God will rejoice over Jerusalem, with whom he is triumphantly and lovingly reunited. And Jerusalem shall be famed and praised by the peoples of the world.

This last section of the book marks a reversal of previous parts, especially 1:10–16: the noise of battle and defeat becomes the sound of celebration and triumph; God the destructive warrior is now the protector; the searching out for purposes of punishment turns into the gathering in for renewal. Fortunes are restored. All of the main "characters"—God, Israel, and the nations—who earlier were bringing judgment or suffering destruction are here joined together in benevolence in this vision of comfort. The creation which was to have been swept away is reaffirmed.

This message of comfort shares the tone and language of Jeremiah 33 and Deutero-Isaiah.

Subject Index

♦

AUTHOR INDEX

◆

INDEX OF SCRIPTURAL
REFERENCES

◆